Contents

Section 1 Suggested answers to activities in the students' book

Unit 1 Meat, fish and eggs	2
Case Study The Co-op and egg production	3
Unit 2 Dairy products	4
Unit 3 Vegetable foods	6
Unit 4 Fats and oils	8
Unit 5 Sugar	9
Case Study Cane sugar processing at Tate & Lyle	9
Unit 6 Nutrients	11
Case Study Marketing meat substitutes	12
Case Study Fortification of food	13
Unit 7 Dietary Reference Values	14
Unit 8 Meal planning	15
Case Study Assessing school meals	16
Unit 9 Food hygiene	17
Case Study Food hygiene at Safeway	17
Unit 10 Food preservation	18
Unit 11 Additives	20
Case Study Food labelling	20
Case Study Additives	21
Case Study Extended life milk	21
Unit 12 Healthy eating	22
Unit 13 Illness and disorders	24
Case Study Tesco's Healthy Eating campaign	24
Case Study Parkwood House Day Nursery	25
Unit 14 Food materials	26
Unit 15 Measurement and proportion	27
Case Study Bramley's Coffee House	28
Case Study Measurement at British Bakeries	28
Unit 16 Adapting recipes	29
Unit 17 Cooking food	31
Unit 18 Mixing, cutting, forming and shaping	33
Unit 19 Using tools safely	35
Case Study The Hotwich	36
Case Study Dangerous machines	36
Case Study Making pasta	37
Unit 20 Large equipment	38
Unit 21 Presentation and finishing techniques	40
Case Study Elro tilting pressure bratt pan	40
Case Study Heathcotes Brasserie	41
Unit 22 Product development	42
Case Study Product development at Birds Eye	44
Case Study The wonder bean?	44
Unit 23 Sensory analysis	45
Unit 24 Disassembly	46
Unit 25 Packaging	47
Case Study Kellogg's Corn Flakes	48
Case Study Design and packaging at Cadbury	49
Unit 26 Planning work	50
Unit 27 Working economically	51
Case Study Film Cuisine	52
Case Study Automatic replenishment at United Biscuits	53
Unit 28 Systems	54
Unit 29 Quality	55
Case Study Pizza production	55
Case Study Heygates flour mill	56
Unit 30 The law and the food industry	57
Unit 31 Risk assessment	58
Case Study Designing hygienic kitchens	59
Case Study HACCP at Burnaby Hospital	59

Section 2 Planned activities for Design and Technology - Food

Introduction	60
Lesson scheme - All about sauces	61
Teaching matrix 1 - Fruit and vegetables	84
Teaching matrix 2 - Yeast products	88
Teaching matrix 3 - Burgers, meat and fish	92
Teaching matrix 4 - Chilled products/Eggs and dairy foods	96
Teaching matrix 5 - Alternatives to meat and fish	100
Teaching matrix 6 - New product development/Food as material	104

Section 3 Reference material

Introduction	108
Research sheets	
Questionnaires	110
Comparison sheets	112
Technology process sheets	
Product specification	114
Evaluating existing products	115
Recipe development and evaluation	116
Organisation and management	117
Hygiene and safety procedures	118
Evaluation help sheet 1	119
Evaluation help sheet 2	120
Practical planners	
Shopping order	122
Recipe planner	123
Costing sheet	124
Planning sheets	
Visual design planner 1	125
Visual design planner 2	126
Design planner	127
Data analysis sheets	
Table	128
Nutrition information chart	129
Food facts	130
Blank charts and guides	
Brainstorm charts	131
Planning schedule	133
Flow chart	134
Pie chart	135
Menu blank	136
Menu fonts	137
Lines - portrait	138
Lines - landscape	139
KS4 Design and Technology mapping pro forma	140

Section 4 Product and business index

	141

Section 1

Unit 1: Meat, fish and eggs

Suggested answers

Activities page 3

1. Two reasons why meat turns brown:
- Meat browns at temperatures above 65°C.
- The pigment myoglobin browns when heated.
- The reaction between sugars and amino acids or proteins produces brown pigments. This type of browning is sometimes described as the Maillard reaction, after the Frenchman who discovered how it happened.

2. Suggested chicken dishes for staff canteen:
- Breaded boned chicken pieces **deep fried** and served with a salad.
- Chicken casserole **(oven)**. Jointed chicken pieces, cooked in a mushroom sauce and served with a selection of fresh vegetables.
- Curried chicken **(hob)**. Chicken pieces cooked in a curry sauce and served with rice.

Suggested lamb dishes for staff canteen:
- Lamb chops **(grilled)**, and served with a selection of fresh vegetables.
- **Roast** saddle of lamb, served with a selection of fresh vegetables.
- Braised shoulder of lamb **(oven)**. Meat is cooked on a bed of chopped vegetables, e.g. carrots, leeks, onions and garlic. The meat is partially covered with stock and cooked in a closed dish. The vegetables may be used to make an accompanying sauce. Served with a selection of fresh vegetables.

3. Design a questionnaire to find out meat eating habits.
Any suitable questionnaire which is designed to enable students to answer the questions listed. A photocopiable example is given on p. 111. Students could use the tally method for recording answers (four ticks and a line through = five answers). This method is easy to complete and can be totalled rapidly. Students could present their results as a bar chart.

Activities page 4

1. Why is white fish a useful food for a person trying to lose weight?
White fish contains almost no fat. Fish protein contains a higher level of water than meat, therefore gram for gram fish contains less protein than meat. The Western diet tends to include more protein than is necessary for health in the daily intake. Excess protein will be used as energy food, and thereafter laid down as fat. Cutting down on meat eating and increasing on white fish could therefore assist in weight loss.

2. How should a restaurant store the following fish and fish dishes?

a) and b) Fresh trout/mackerel
Store in refrigerator for 1-2 days, freezer for 2/3 months. Store separately, ideally in a separate refrigerator. Store in a box containing ice, at a temperature of 1-2°C. Boxes should be clearly labelled so that no confusion arises when portions are removed from the refrigerator for preparation.

c) Prepared cod mornay
Store in refrigerator for 1-2 days, freezer for up to 2 months. Cooked fish should be stored above raw fish in the refrigerator to prevent cross-contamination. If not intended to be used on the day of preparation, the dish could be preserved using sous-vide (see Unit 10).

d) Prawn cocktail
The ingredients for a prawn cocktail should be assembled only when ordered. It is not advisable to leave the completed dish in the refrigerator for any length of time, as the sauce used could sink away from the prawns, and will also make lettuce soggy. There is a danger of cross-contamination if portioned dishes are left open on refrigerator shelves. Cooked prawns should be stored on the top shelves of a refrigerator for 1-2 days. Prawns may be frozen for up to 2 months. Prawn cocktail is not suitable for freezing.

GCSE Design and Technology

Food Technology

Teachers' guide

CLIFF PARK HIGH SCHOOL
(GRANT MAINTAINED)

Celia Barker
Sue Kimmings
Charmian Phillips

CAUSEWAY PRESS

Preface

GCSE Design and Technology - Food Technology Teachers' Guide is designed to be photocopied within the purchaser's institution and copyright is waived. It is hoped that the guide will provide a valuable source of information and act as a flexible teaching resource that will save vital preparation time. It is divided into four sections.

- Section 1 contains suggested answers to all activities and case studies that appear in the students' book. These answers are only suggestions; there are other possible answers, but space prevents their inclusion.

- Section 2 contains planned activities for Design and Technology - Food, including design briefs, lesson plans, differentiated questions and suggested answers.

- Section 3 contains reference material, including guides, charts and tables. These photocopiable pro formas help to back up activities in the students' book and will save preparation time.

- Section 4 is an index of products and businesses that appear in the students' book. This will help students searching for references to particular food products or businesses and is particularly useful for commodity based project work.

Celia Barker
Sue Kimmings
Charmian Phillips

British Library Cataloguing in Publication Data
A catalogue record for this book is available from the British Library.

ISBN 1-873929-64-1

Cover design	Caroline Waring-Collins
Cover photograph	Telegraph Colour Library
Reader	Annemarie Work
Editor	Lisa Fabry

Causeway Press Limited
PO Box 13, Ormskirk, Lancashire L39 5HP
© Celia Barker, Sue Kimmings and Charmian Phillips
1st impression 1997
Reprinted 1998

Origination and layout by Waring Collins Partnership, Ormskirk, Lancashire
Printed and bound by Redwood Books, Trowbridge

Suggested answers — unit 1

Activities page 6

1. What happens when eggs are heated?
The whole egg. The egg white begins to coagulate at 60°C, when the protein ovalbumin begins to separate out as a solid. As the temperature rises, coagulation continues until the whole egg is solid.
A beaten egg combined with milk will coagulate, when cooked over a gentle heat, to form a thickened sauce or custard.
When **egg white** is beaten, partial coagulation of the ovalbumin occurs as the egg foams. When this foam is heated it becomes rigid as the protein continues to coagulate further. Addition of sugar strengthens the foam by absorbing the water in the egg white and reducing the possibility of the foam collapsing.

2. Give three egg dishes and the function the egg performs.
Any suitable answer, for example:
- Egg custard tart - the egg **thickens** the milk, producing a soft set filling in a pastry case.
- Lemon meringue pie - egg white is **aerated** (whisked) and sugar is added to form a meringue. Egg yolk is used to **thicken** the lemon filling.
- Fruit cake - the egg holds air to make the cake light and **binds** the ingredients together.
- Scotch egg - a **hard boiled** egg is covered with sausage meat and then **egg and breadcrumbed** prior to deep frying.
- Apple fritters - sliced apple rings are **coated** in a sweet batter and deep fried.
- Brioche - a soft sweet French bread which is **glazed** before cooking to give a shiny golden finish.

3. Design a leaflet on buying and storing eggs.
An opportunity for students to carry out an extended design activity, using the information contained in the unit. The leaflet can be designed by hand or on a computer, but must contain original artwork by students.

Case Study
The Co-op and egg production

Activities page 7

1. Three main systems of egg production:
- Battery
- Barn/Perchery
- Free Range.

2. Battery system considered more efficient because:
- more hens can be housed per square metre
- feed and water can be controlled by computer programming to each cage
- eggs can be collected with greater ease as they drop outside the cage into troughs
- the system is a cost efficient way of producing large quantities of eggs.

3. Factors which might influence purchase of eggs produced using a particular system:
- **Cost**
  Battery eggs cost least and offer a cheap source of protein for people on a limited budget. Barn eggs cost less than Free Range. Free Range eggs are the most expensive.
- **Well-being of chickens**
  Free Range and Barn/Perchery producers give greater consideration to the well-being of the birds.
- **Taste**
  Many consumers believe that Free Range eggs taste better than others. This has not been proved scientifically.

4. Effect of labelling eggs as 'Intensively Produced' on buying habits of consumers.
Students may discuss some of the following issues.
- Customers can now choose which production method they prefer.
- Customers who were previously unaware of production method may consider this issue for the first time.
- Customers may be confused by different labels. Store may need to provide additional information about different production systems.
- Store can monitor which types of egg are popular in different areas. This will inform store of how concerned customers are about methods of egg production and will allow store to deliver preferred eggs to different branches.

5. Advantages of date stamping eggs:
- age easily checked
- good stock rotation.

As eggs can be a source of salmonella poisoning, it is important that they are not used after the recommended use by date.

Dairy products

Suggested answers

Activities page 8

Which type of milk suitable for:

1. Family with 3 year old
The full cream milk bought in bulk from the supermarket. This milk is often cheaper than milk delivered to the door.

2. Camping
UHT milk which is easy to pack and store before use. The container is light and easy to dispose of after use. Once opened, UHT milk must be used and stored as fresh milk.

3. Elderly person
Bottled milk delivered to the door, ensuring a regular supply and allowing the person to purchase other food products stocked by the milkman.

4. Teenager wanting to lose weight
Skimmed milk which is low in fat, but high in calcium.

Activities page 8

1. a) Why people have milk delivered to doorstep.
Students could suggest any of the following reasons.
- Convenient for the customer, who does not have to carry a heavy item from the supermarket.
- May be friendly, personal service.
- Milkman often offers a range of other goods.
- Regular delivery is often more convenient for elderly, housebound and disabled people and also offers contact with the outside world. Milkmen are often the first to realise if something is wrong when the bottle remains on the step.

b) Why people buy milk from shops/supermarkets.
Students could suggest any of the following reasons.
- Often cheaper than doorstep delivery.
- Milk available in 568ml (1 pint), 1.136 litres (2 pints), 2.272 litres (4 pints), and 3.4 litres (6 pints) plastic containers. These containers can be frozen which means that people are able to store enough milk for their needs each week or month.
- People can purchase milk as and when they need it, rather than having a regular order with the milkman which can either be too much or not enough depending on family consumption from day to day.
- Containers can be thrown away after use with no need for rinsing before disposal.

2. Advantages and disadvantages of various forms of milk packaging.

Bottles
ADVANTAGES: Can be recycled about 20 times and so are environmentally friendly.
DISADVANTAGES: Expensive initial cost. Heavy, so expensive to transport. May be broken during transportation or use.

Cartons
ADVANTAGES: Treated card which holds liquid safely and hygienically. Light, good shape for storing. Card can be burned after use or will be biodegradable so is environmentally friendly. Inexpensive form of packaging.
DISADVANTAGES: Fragile, can be damaged during transportation or use. Cartons can be difficult to open.

Plastic bottles/containers
ADVANTAGES: Light and easy to carry. Can be squashed down after use before disposal. A triangular recycling sign indicates if the plastic is recyclable.
DISADVANTAGES: More expensive than cartons. Some plastics are not biodegradable and can take up to five hundred years to disintegrate!

Activities page 10

1. Brainstorm types of yogurt.
You could use the brainstorm charts on pp. 131-2 for this activity. As an example of the types of yogurt available, this is a selection of yogurts displayed in Tesco 26/11/96.

Tesco own brand:
Tesco Bio, virtually fat free
Tesco virtually fat free
Tesco smooth set, French style, low fat
Tesco Fabulously Fruity

Suggested answers   unit 2

Tesco Greek style, thick and creamy
Tesco Custard style Crumble Corner - strawberry
Tesco whole milk - summer fruits and berries
Tesco Thick and Creamy, fruit plus yogurt.

Other makes:
Muller Light, low fat
Muller Fruit Corner, thick and creamy
Shape, very low fat
Weight Watchers Yogurt by Heinz
Onken Bio Pot, whole grain
Ski, low fat
Ski Fruit Split, low fat.

2. Other target groups.
Students could suggest a range of different customers, in addition to children and slimmers, for example, those:
- who require a high fibre content
- who want a low fat food
- who want a 'luxury' creamy dessert.
- who have small children (yogurt is useful during the weaning period, and a good source of calcium for growing children).

Activities page 11

1. Mozarella is a good choice for pizza because it:
- has a mild flavour, allowing other flavours through
- melts easily
- is elastic, holding other toppings in place and is tender and chewy
- is low in fat/high in moisture so does not burn at high temperatures
- grates easily, and does not clump after grating.

2. How could the company save time and money using mozzarella?
Suggestions might include:
- The quality of grating easily and not sticking after grating helps to ensure that the cheese can be easily measured for each pizza. The same weight must be placed on each pizza to ensure economy for the company, and customer satisfaction with a consistent result each time.
- The high moisture content prevents burning of cheese which could occur if other cheeses were used. This reduces possible waste.
- The low fat content prevents pools of grease collecting which could damage the flavour and texture of the base and other toppings, causing waste.
- The good elasticity keeps other toppings in place, preventing waste.

3. Mozzarella could be suitable for dishes where melt, stretch and texture are important, for example:
- used in a sauce in a pasta dish (e.g. tagliatelle with mozzarella and asparagus sauce)
- used as part of a kebab
- used for toasting (e.g. bruschetta)
- used for melting (e.g. baked aubergines with tomatoes and cheese).

Mozzarella would be unsuitable for dishes that require a strong cheese flavour such as:
- cauliflower cheese
- cheese flan
- cheese pastry.

Unit 3 Vegetable foods

Suggested answers

Activities page 13

1. a) Which cereals have students eaten?
Trigger suggestions:

- **Wheat** - Used as a basis for bread, flour, pasta, biscuits, pastries and cakes. Many ready to eat breakfast cereals are made from wheat, e.g. Puffed Wheat, Wheat Flakes, Shredded Wheat. The bran from wheat is also used for high fibre cereals such as All Bran. **Semolina** is made from durum wheat, grown in Canada, United States and Russia. It is produced in the early stages of milling, when the endosperm is separated from the bran and germ. Used mainly for milk puddings.

- **Rice** - Brown, basmati, long grain, short or round grain, pre-cooked, boil in bag, frozen, easy cook. Can be used in both savoury and sweet dishes. Associated particularly with Chinese, Indian, Italian and Spanish dishes. **Ground rice** is used to thicken soups, and as a dessert. It will also make flour mixtures shorter which is useful in biscuits and some cakes. Rice is also used as a breakfast cereal, e.g. Rice Krispies and in rice pudding.

- **Barley** - **Malt product**s are derived from barley. These are useful for the brewing industry and for malted breads. **Pearl barley** is used to thicken soups and stews. **Barley water** is a soft drink.

- **Maize** - Can be eaten as a vegetable, i.e. corn on the cob. If tinned or frozen, this is more often referred to as **sweetcorn**. **Cornflour** is made from maize - it thickens sauces and is added to biscuits and cakes to aid shortening. Maize is also used in breakfast cereals, e.g. corn flakes. It can also be used for snacks such as corn chips, tortillas and popcorn.

- **Oats** - Rolled oats are used for porridge, flapjacks and muesli. **Oatmeal** is used for porridge, haggis, parkin and oatcakes.

- **Rye** - Used for crispbreads, and a heavy, dark bread popular in Scandinavian countries and Russia where the cereal grows.

b) Which is most commonly eaten cereal in Britain?
Wheat.

Suggestions for food products containing wheat might include:
- plain flour
- wholemeal flour
- pasta
- wholemeal bread
- pitta bread
- pastry
- crumpets
- biscuits
- sponge fingers
- doughnuts
- Danish pastries
- breakfast cereal.

2. a) What happens to flour when it is cooked?
When making a roux, the starch grains are moistened and heated. This causes them to thicken in a process called gelatinisation. When the flour is added to the melted butter, the starch granules in the flour become coated with fat and some gelatinisation of the starch will occur. However, until the liquid is added, and further heat applied to the sauce, most of the starch granules will remain uncooked. As the heat increases, the starch gelatinises, and thickens the mixture producing a smooth glossy sauce.

b) What could go wrong when making roux? How could you overcome problems?
Suggestions might include:
- Liquid is added too quickly and the sauce is lumpy. Correct by using a liquidiser.
- Sauce is too thick because liquid has been added over the heat or incorrect proportions of flour to liquid have been used.
- Sauce is too thin because incorrect proportions of flour to liquid have been used.
- The sauce has a poor flavour because the roux (the butter and flour mixture) has been burned, giving a slightly bitter taste and colouring the sauce.
- The sauce has a poor colour because the roux has been burned or a metal spoon has been used to stir the sauce.
- Use a wooden spoon for a good coloured sauce and for safety.

Activities page 14

1. What types of pulse are used in recipe?
Butter or haricot beans, green lentils.

Suggested answers
unit 3

2. Which ingredients supply:
a) protein?
- haricot and butter beans
- lentils
- nuts
- egg
- oats
- green pepper (trace)
- onion (trace)
- carrot (trace).

b) NSP?
- haricot and butter beans
- lentils
- oats
- nuts
- carrots
- onion.

3. Plan work schedule for preparing recipe. It is suggested that a time plan sheet is used.
Table 1 shows one way of producing a time plan.

Activities page 16

1. Suggest ways of conserving vitamin C:
- where possible use vegetables raw
- do not peel, or pare very thinly as vitamin is stored near skin
- never leave vegetables soaking in water as vitamin C is water soluble
- cook for shortest time possible, using minimum of water
- where possible use water in which vegetables were cooked (e.g. stock, gravy)
- buy vegetables/fruit regularly - vitamin C is lost as they age.

2. Suggest low fat recipes using potatoes.
Potatoes which have been boiled or baked are healthiest. Many people like chips but the fat content is high. Chips fried in vegetable oil are healthier than chips fried in animal fat. Thin chips absorb most oil. Thicker chips have less surface area to absorb fat. Fat content of commercially prepared chips: oven (5%), ordinary (10%), thin cut (20%).

Suggestions for recipes might include:
- jacket potatoes with a low fat filling (e.g. baked beans, cottage cheese)
- roast potatoes (parboil potatoes, score with fork, sprinkle with Lo Salt and roast in a dry baking tin until golden and crispy)
- potato and mushroom gratin (parboil potatoes, slice and layer with mushrooms, onions and low fat fromage frais, bake until tender and golden).

Activities page 17

1. Why might parents choose Pure Fruit?
Suggestions might include:
- low in fat and salt
- no added sugar
- good energy source
- attractive packaging
- easy to store and use.

2. Why does Pure Fruit come in a variety of flavours?
Suggestions might include:
- introduce children to a variety of tastes
- if children do not like one flavour, there are alternatives.

3. Children to avoid sugar and salt. Is Pure Fruit suitable?
Pure Fruit contains only a trace of sodium. It contains 11.2g of sugars per 100g but these are natural fruit sugars, and in about the same quantities as a fresh apple.

4. What proportion of baby's energy needs is supplied by pot of Pure Fruit?
Baby needs 865kcal
90g pot = 44 kcal

$$\frac{44\text{kcal}}{865\text{kcal}} \times 100 = 5\% \text{ daily needs}$$

Table 1		
Time	**Action**	**Special Points**
Evening before	Put the dried beans to soak.	
3.30pm	Drain beans, rinse lentils, place in saucepan, cover with stock and bring to boil. Simmer until tender.	
3.35pm	Prepare onion, carrots and peppers.	
3.45pm	Fry onion until soft, add carrot, pepper and nuts and cook gently for a further 5-6 minutes. Season.	
5.15pm	Drain lentils and purée. Stir into the vegetable mixture.	
5.20pm	Leave mixture to cool in refrigerator. Wash up.	
5.40pm	Egg and coat the patties and put oil on to heat on a gentle heat.	
5.45pm	Place patties in the pan to cook.	Ensure the oil is at the correct temperature.
5.50pm	Turn the patties over.	Use a fish slice.
5.55pm	Remove patties from the pan, drain and serve.	

Suggested answers

Unit 4 Fats and oils

Activities page 19

1. Suggest a fat or oil suitable for following tasks:

a) pastry for a sweet tart
butter for flavour, hard margarine with lard for economy and addition of vitamin D, hard vegetable margarine for vegetarians.

b) dressing for green salad
olive oil or nut oils e.g. walnut for flavour, blended vegetable oils for economy.

c) deep frying doughnuts
vegetable oil to produce high enough temperature for frying without decomposition.

d) shallow frying fish
butter for flavour or vegetable oil to produce high enough temperature for frying without decomposition.

2. a) Health reasons for choosing Mono instead of butter:
- Mono is lower in saturated fat which has been linked to cholesterol build up and heart disease (see Unit 6)
- Mono has a higher proportion of monounsaturates and polyunsaturates, which are considered to be healthier forms of fat - they do not raise blood cholesterol level and may even reduce it.

b) What is hydrogenated oil?
Hydrogen is pumped into oil which changes the size of the molecules resulting in a solid fat which has a soft spreadable consistency. These are called trans fats. This process causes unsaturated fats to become more like saturated fats (see Unit 6).

c) Suggest recipes using Mono.
Mono could be used for spreading, shallow frying or baking. It cannot be used for deep frying.
Suitable suggestions might include:
- a spread for bread
- shallow frying fish cakes
- sauce for cauliflower cheese
- Victoria Sandwich
- crumble topping.

8

unit 5 Sugar

Activities page 20

1. Table 2 shows some further examples for each property of sugar.

Table 2

PROPERTY	EXAMPLE
CONTRIBUTES TO:	
sweetness	cakes, biscuits
viscosity	sweetened fruit purée
volume	Soufflé
texture	Toffee, fudge
ENHANCES:	
flavour	new potatoes, peas, duck
appearance	crystallised fruits, cake decorations
INCREASES:	
moisture retention	creamed mixtures, e.g.
boiling point	fruit cakes
	syrups, jams
ASSISTS:	
emulsification	mayonnaise, rich cake
colour development	mixture, bread, pastry
fermentation	breadmaking, wine and beer production
DELAYS:	
staling	biscuits
discolouration	poached fruits
lowers freezing point	sorbet
inhibits mould growth	sweet pickles, chutney

2. In what ways is sugar useful to baker?
Suggestions might include:
- sweetens cakes and biscuits
- aids fermentation of yeast mixtures
- used as a glaze on sticky buns
- fondant icings on iced buns
- fondant and royal icings on celebration cakes
- caramel icings.

3. **What properties of sugar help in making preserves?**
When pectin is mixed with the right proportions of acid and sugar in preserve making, the mixture will set and gel. The presence of the sugar **inhibits mould growth** in the jam. Sugar **contributes to sweetness, viscosity and texture** and **enhances the flavour and appearance** of jams and chutneys.

Case Study
Cane sugar processing at Tate & Lyle

Activities page 21

1. By-products of cane sugar processing and their uses:
- **cane molasses**, used by the food industry and as animal feed
- **bagasse**, used to fuel sugar mills and to make paper
- **bagasse** ash from boilers, used as fertiliser.

2. a) Main products of sugar cane:
- **white sugars** - granulated, caster, icing, preserving, sugar lumps
- **raw brown sugar**s - demerara (e.g. Mauritian or Barbados), light and dark Muscovado sugars
- **refined brown sugars** - light and dark soft brown sugars
- **golden syrup**
- **treacle**
- **molasses.**

b) Stages at which products are extracted:

Stage 1 - the cane sugar factory
- **raw sugar** - produced after crystallisation and separation by centrifuge
- **molasses** - the liquor spun from the centrifuge.

Stage 2 - the refinery
- **white sugars** - extracted after centifugal separation in Stage 2
- **syrup, treacle and soft brown sugar** - made from syrups remaining after white sugar has been produced

- **refinery molasses** is the end product of the refining process when it is no longer economically practical to extract any more white sugar.

Other products are typically produced by secondary processing, e.g.
- cubes are granulated sugar, moistened, pressed and re-dried
- icing sugar is granulated sugar milled to a fine size
- refined soft brown sugars are caster sugar blended with specially clarified molasses
- golden syrup is made from liquors produced during the refining process.

3. This activity provides an opportunity for students to carry out an extended research, writing and design activity. Students should have access to resources to enable them to find out the information needed to complete this activity. It may help less able students if you ask them to model their answer on the Case Study (i.e. a short written introduction, followed by a detailed annotated diagram).

unit 6

Nutrients

Activities page 23

Suggest day's menu for following people, focusing on including sufficient protein intake.
Note to teachers, all groups to have breakfast. Students should take into account the following factors whenn planning menus.

CARMEL - daily protein requirement 51g
Also ensure enough:
- calcium and iron for growing foetus
- folic acid for prevention of spina bifida
- fibre to prevent constipation
- complex carbohydrate for energy

and limit fat, sugar and salt intake.

RORY - daily protein requirement 14.5g
Also ensure enough:
- calcium
- complex carbohydrate for energy

and limit sweet foods which could lead to sweet tooth/tooth decay. Whole milk should be given up to age 5.

Ideas for packed lunch:
- wholemeal bread for sandwiches
- cereal bars as alternative to sweets
- yogurt or fromage frais
- fresh or dried fruit

KEN - daily protein requirement 42.6g
- ensure enough complex carbohydrate for energy
- high energy breakfast required
- packed lunches or bought snacks as alternatives
- limit fat
- avoid too much sugar which will provide instant yet short-term energy.

Activities page 25

1. How do simple and complex carbohydrates differ?

Simple carbohydrates
- known as sugars
- chemically called monosaccharides
- e.g. glucose and fructose.

Complex carbohydrates
- non-sweet carbohydrates
- chemically known as polysaccharides
- complicated molecular structure
- e.g. starch and NSP.

2. Problems caused by having a 'sweet tooth' (a preference for sweet foods):
- tooth decay
- excessive intake of energy - could lead to obesity and diabetes.

3. Staple foods from other cultures.
Suggestions might include:
rice - Asia
pasta - Italy
yam - West Indies.

4. Carbohydrates to reduce in our diet.
Extrinsic and non-milk extrinsic sugars (e.g. table sugar and sweetened processed products).

Carbohydrates to increase in our diet.
Complex carbohydrates (e.g. potatoes, rice, pasta, bread).

5. Why might some people be reluctant to increase complex carbohydrate in diet?
- fear of becoming overweight (unfounded)
- possible dislike of texture of wholemeal pasta and brown rice
- unwillingness to increase vegetable and fruit content of diet.

6. a) Carbohydrate bar chart
Should indicate the total carbohydrate content of the cereal, i.e. the sugar and fibre figures combined.

b) Which cereal suitable for:

6 year old?
- students may suggest cereals aimed at children (Sugar Puffs, Frosties, Coco Pops, Rice Krispies, Cheerios) - raise awareness of sugar and fibre content in these samples.
- Weetabix or Quaker Oats are good low sugar, high fibre alternatives.

Aerobics teacher?
- high energy product is required
- cereals with high NSP content will act as a filler
- good choices - Cheerios, Weetabix, Shredded Wheat, All

unit 6 — Suggested answers

Bran, Bran Hearts and Quaker Oats
- Note how sugar added at table will affect energy content.

Slimmer?
- look for low sugar brands
- cereals with high NSP content will act as a filler
- note how sugar added at the table can alter calorie content - raise awareness of alternative sweeteners, e.g. fresh fruit or artificial sweetener
- good choices - All Bran, Weetabix, Shredded Wheat, Quaker Oats and corn flakes.

Activities page 26

1. Reasons for reducing fat:
- can lead to obesity
- danger of heart disease.

2. Argument for retaining some dietary fat:
- some fat is needed for cholesterol production
- adds variety and flavour to foods
- gives a feeling of satiety (being full up).

3. Modification of recipes to reduce saturated fat.
Suggestions might include:
- low fat spread in pastry
- vegetable oil for frying chips
- fruit salad with low fat fromage frais or yogurt.

Activities page 27

1. Need for folic acid before pregnancy.
Helps to ensure that foetus is protected in the first 12 weeks of pregnancy when baby most at risk from neural tube defects.

2. Conservation of folic acid.
B vitamins are water soluble and destroyed by heat, overcooking and storage, therefore:
- do not soak vegetables in water
- cook for the minimum amount of time
- use fresh foods.

3. Plan a day's menus for a pregnant woman.
Trigger ideas:
- use vegetarian cookery books
- include interesting and unusual salads
- include dishes using cereals.

Activities page 29

1. Plan menu including vitamin A in each meal.
- pupils to consider 3 meals
- could sort vitamin A rich foods into appropriate groups for breakfast, lunch and dinner then use cookery books to suggest recipes.

2. Two groups who need vitamin D.
Suggestions might include:
- children
- elderly people
- pregnant women
- breastfeeding women.

Reason for regular supply:
- helps absorb calcium
- formation of bones and teeth
- healing of bones.

3. Conserving vitamin C.
Vitamin C is water soluble and destroyed by air, heat, and cooking, therefore:
- do not soak vegetables in water
- avoid lengthy cooking
- do not cut or chop vegetables too small
- use fresh foods/do not store for too long.

4. Mineral deficiency noted by the dentist.
Calcium and/or phosphorous shown by deteriorating teeth.

5. Anaemia.
Lack of iron. When suggesting meals, students should remember:
- include meat, fish, egg yolk, pulses, cereals, dried fruit, green vegetables
- vtamin C helps absorption of iron
- some kinds of NSP inhibit absorption of iron.

Case Study
Marketing meat substitutes

Activities page 30

1. Reasons for eating mycoprotein.
Suggestions might include:
- vegetarian (but see answer to 3)
- require a low fat diet
- require more fibre in diet
- require more protein in diet
- increase variety in diet
- aware of environmental issues, e.g. cost and intensity of meat rearing.

2. Design a flow chart showing stages in the production of mycoprotein.
Stages in flow chart could be:
1. Growth of fungus in fermentation tower
2. Addition of oxygen, nitrogen, glucose, vitamins and minerals

Suggested answers   unit 6

3. Heat treatment
4. Filtering
5. Draining
6. Addition of egg albumen
7. Flavouring and colouring
8. Texturing
9. Shredding, chopping and slicing.

3. Is Quorn suitable for vegetarians?
The egg albumen used comes from battery eggs. This means that the Vegetarian Society will not award its seal of approval. Some vegetarians may choose to eat Quorn despite this.

4. Suggestions for Quorn dishes.
Quorn can be substituted for meat in any recipe.

5. Why do we need new sources of protein?
Suggestions might include:
- environmental issues
- expense of meat production
- growing population
- growing number of vegetarians.

Case Study
Fortification of food

Activities page 31

1. Nutritional analysis of homemade versus tinned pasta.
Students could use the pro forma on p. 129. Students should compare the following:
- energy
- protein
- carbohydrate
- fat
- NSP
- sodium.

2. Reasons for fortification of food.
Suggestions might include:
- to ensure everyone receives adequate amounts of some vitamins and minerals
- to create a value added product
- to replace nutrients lost during processing.

3. a) Improving NSP content of home made pasta with tomato sauce.
Suggestions might include:
- use wholewheat pasta
- add chick peas or lentils to sauce
- accompany with a salad.

b) Improving NSP content of Heinz spaghetti in tomato sauce.
Suggestions might include:
- serve on wholemeal bread
- accompany with jacket potato.

4. Product comparison.
Students could use the pro forma on p. 112.

Unit 7: Dietary Reference Values

Suggested answers

Activities page 32

1. EAR for vitamin C for people over 15.
25 mg per day.

2. Vitamin C requirement for breastfeeding women.
The EAR is 55 mg per day. However, to ensure that this mother meets her individual requirement (which could be higher than the average), it would be advisable for her to consume the RNI of 70mg daily. This could be obtained from fresh fruit (especially citrus fruits) vegetables or supplements.

3. Vitamin C requirement in school lunches.
In order to meet the needs of all age groups within a school, it is advisable to include a vitamin C content of 40 mg, which is the RNI for people aged 15 and over.

4. Is average intake of 22mg adequate for group of 8 year olds?
The children need to increase the amount of vitamin C in their diet. The EAR for a group of 8 year olds is 20mg vitamin C. However, this is only an average. Some children may need less than this amount. Some may need more. To ensure that everyone in a group receives an adequate intake of vitamin C, it is advisable that the average intake meets the RNI of 30mg.

Activities page 33

1. What do the figures in the table tell you about:
a) changing energy needs from birth to 18?
For both boys and girls, there is a steady increase in energy requirement during this period. Boys require more kcals than girls.

b) Change in energy requirements between 18 and 75?
There is a steady decline between 18 and 75.

c) Different energy needs of men and women?
Men have a larger energy requirement.

2. Who needs more energy, a woman of 17 or a man aged 77?
The woman has a fractionally higher energy requirement than the man (2,110 kcals/day for the woman; 2,100 for the man).

3. How many kcals does 2 year old boy need daily? What else is important when planning his diet?
Tom requires 1,230 kcals daily. Other factors to bear in mind when feeding a toddler might include:
- give full fat milk and other dairy products for energy and vitamins
- meals should provide protein for growth
- ensure adequate intake of vitamins and minerals
- there should be adequate but not excessive amounts of NSP (a diet high in NSP can inhibit the digestion of other nutrients)
- no whole nuts should be given (risk of choking); chopped or ground nuts should be given with care (because the child may show an allergy)
- give small, regular meals and healthy snacks
- the amount of non-milk extrinsic sugars in a toddler's diet should be limited
- there should be a variety of flavours and textures to make the meal appealing to a child.

Meal planning

Activities page 34

1. Suggest three quick and healthy meals from ingredients listed.

Suggestions might include:
- bread with cheese and tomatoes
- baked beans on toast and fresh fruit
- yogurt with dried fruit
- chicken curry with stir-fried rice and vegetables
- stewed apple with yogurt
- mushroom omelette with corn and tomatoes
- pizza and fresh fruit salad.

Students should remember to include a variety of nutrients, colours and textures within each meal.

Activities page 35

1. Suggest meals to help overcome problems.

a) Young child does not like milk.
Supply recipes where milk is disguised, such as sauces (e.g. lasagne), quiches, puddings (e.g. rice pudding). Compensate for possible lack of milk in the diet by feeding cheese and yogurt.

b) Lacto-vegetarian worried about eating enough vitamin B12.
Will obtain from milk, eggs, cheese, yeast extract and soya products.

c) Manual worker eating diet high in fat.
Charlie's diet is too high in fat. He should substitute long term high energy foods such as rice, pasta and bread.
Suggested dishes might be:
- pizza with salad and a jacket potato
- chicken risotto
- steamed sponge pudding
- spaghetti bolognese with garlic bread
- fresh fruit salad containing bananas.

d) Man with limited mobility becomes constipated.
Constipation occurs through lack of exercise and inadequate amounts of NSP. Arthur needs foods which can be bought for him by a helper and stored, e.g. canned beans, dried pulses and wholemeal cereals.

Suggested meals might be:
- mixed bean curry
- vegetable pie with wholemeal pastry
- wholemeal pasta with tomato sauce.

e) Pregnant woman uncomfortable after meals.
Nell needs small frequent meals that will not fill her up too much.
Suggested meals might include:
- homemade soups
- jacket potatoes with fillings
- wholemeal cereals with milk
- fresh fruit salad and yogurt.

Her diet may become more snack orientated towards the end of her pregnancy. She should avoid too many sweet or fatty foods.

2. Suggest ways of preparing ingredients suggested for different groups.

a) 14 year old trying to lose weight.
Microwave cooked fish in parsley sauce (made with low fat spread and skimmed milk). Fruit flan rather than pie to reduce amount of pastry. Water, fresh orange juice or low calorie cold drink.

b) Active 71 year old man.
Fried fish with tartare sauce (frying supplies additional kcals). Vegetables well cooked (older people may have chewing problems). Use filo pastry in the dessert as it is lighter and more easily digested. Fresh orange juice (vitamin C often lacking in diet of older people).

c) Faddy toddler.
Fish fingers (grilled) with tomato sauce. Vegetables combined for colour and interest. Individual fruit tart. Fresh fruit juice or fresh banana milkshake.

Activities page 36

1. a) How does restaurant cater for different groups?
Suggestions might include:
- offers range of meat, fish and vegetarian options
- offers simple dishes (e.g. ploughman's, farmer's)
- offers more unusual dishes (e.g. French platter, Greek salad,

unit 8 — Suggested answers

Tuna and bean salad)
- offers low fat option (Lifestyle platter).

b) Comment on choices in terms of healthy eating guidelines.
Suggestions might include:
- variety of foods in each choice
- protein in every choice
- starch and fibre in every choice (bread and salad)
- may be high in fat, depending on dressings or type of cheese
- range of vitamins and minerals supplied
- some chutneys may be high in sugar.

2. Plan and prepare menus for food outlets.
Students should consider the following points:
- who will eat in outlet
- needs of this group
- preferences of this group
- likely budget of this group
- healthy eating guidelines.

Activities page 37

This set of activities offers an opportunity for discussion about the effects of income on diet. The following information may be useful.

The weekly figure of £45 for family of 2 adults and 2 children is based on a low income shopping basket designed for a family of 4 by Sainsbury in 1994, costing £11.66 per person. Even at this modest level, a family on benefits could find it difficult to pay for this shopping basket. In 1994 the average benefit level for a 2 child family was £113.05, so the basket costs nearly 40% of income. In Britain the average family spends 17% of income on food. You may wish to adjust the figure used in this activity to reflect a realistic figure based on current benefit levels.

Case Study: Assessing school meals

Activities page 39

1. Nutritional value of Natalie's average lunchtime meal.
Suggestions might include:
- too many kilocalories
- too much fat, especially saturated fat
- too much sugar
- not enough starch, iron or folate
- good levels of fibre, vitamin A and vitamin C.

2. Changes Natalie could make to improve diet.
Suggestions might include:
- reduce total energy intake by cutting down on fat and sugar
- reduce fat by replacing chips with boiled or baked potatoes
- reduce fat and sugar by replacing puddings, biscuits and chocolate bars with fresh fruit
- increase fibre, vitamins and minerals by eating wholemeal bread, rice and pasta
- increase fibre, vitamins and minerals by eating more fruit and vegetables
- reduce sugar by replacing sweetened drinks with water, milk or unsweetened fruit juices.

3. a) Reasons for fewer children eating school lunch.
Suggestions might include:
- cost of school lunches
- students leaving school premises at lunch time
- quality of school lunches
- preference for packed lunch.

b) Survey to find out what children eat at lunchtime.
Students could use the questionnaire pro forma on p. 110.

4. Advantages and disadvantages of statements.
Hot meal at lunchtime:
- hot school lunch may be more filling, especially in winter
- just because meal is hot does not mean it is nutritionally balanced.

Packed lunch - know what child is eating:
- parent can select foods he/she prefers child to eat
- child may not eat lunch.

Old enough to decide:
- child can choose what he/she likes
- may not choose meal which meets nutritional guidelines.

Packed lunch - favourite foods:
- child likely to eat lunch
- favourite foods may not meet nutritional guidelines.

Food hygiene

Activities page 44

1. Number of reported cases of food poisoning is increasing - suggest reasons.

Suggestions might include:
- public more aware and therefore more likely to report cases
- lifestyle changes - shopping done less often and food stored for longer
- consumer malpractice:
    not following manufacturers' instructions for preparation of product
    not heating or cooking properly
    storing food for too long
    using dirty equipment
    using equipment which is not working satisfactorily
- article argues that much of the food we buy is contaminated with pathogenic bacteria.

2. What precautions should the consumer take to avoid food poisoning?

Consumers should ensure:
- food is heated properly
- food is cooked properly
- manufacturers' preparation instructions are followed
- food is stored correctly
- food preparation surfaces are adequately cleaned.

3. a) - c) Which bacteria mentioned in article, where found and how destroyed?

See Table 3

Table 3

Salmonella	Campylobactes	E coli 0157
eggs, chicken, dairy products, etc.	chickens, raw milk, untreated water	burgers, sausages, processed meat, soft cheese, contaminated water
through cooking	killed above 60°C	killed above 55°C

Case Study
Food hygiene at Safeway

Activities page 45

1. Importance of effective stock rotation.
Items with a shorter use by date are brought to the front and used first.

2. What is the 20 minute rule and why is it important?
Throughout the chill chain, no products must be left out of chill for more than 20 minutes. This rule ensures that products are kept at the correct temperature for most of the time. If they are out of chill, it is for a very short time, which should not affect the safety of a product.

3. What might happen if the temperature in one of the lorries delivering products rose above 7.5°C?
If the lorry is carrying chilled goods, there could be a risk that food has reached an unsafe temperature, and so the delivery load is rejected.

4. How do Safeway staff monitor the temperature in the front of store chilled cabinets and freezers?

Suggestions might include:
- temperature is displayed above each compartment for visual checks
- each compartment is monitored by central computer these temperatures are checked 3 times a day
- alarm sounds if compartment rises above required temperature
- temperature checked by staff using a probe thermometer.

5. State five points to be included in the hygiene training for staff working in the bakery or coffee shop.

Suggestions might include:
- personal hygiene of food handlers
- serving food correctly - using gloves or tongs
- using correct cleaning materials - keeping utensils and surfaces clean
- efficient stock rotation
- temperature control for high risk food products.

Suggested answers

Unit 16 Food preservation

Activities page 46

1. a) **Explain why drying is a successful method of food preservation.**

   Suggestions might include:
   - micro-organisms need water in order to reproduce
   - concentrates the salts and sugars which preserves the food
   - dried foods need no special storage conditions
   - dried foods can be stored for long periods of time.

   b) **Give three situations when dehydrated food could be useful.**

   Suggestions might include:
   - camping holidays - no special storage conditions required
   - single people - as dried food can be reconstituted in small amounts
   - elderly people - dried food is lightweight and easy to transport.

2. **Compare the soup products in Table 1.**

   Students might consider these points:
   - attractiveness (can product be seen through packaging, picture of product on package?)
   - environmental issues (cost of packaging materials, packaging recycled/recyclable?)
   - sensory appeal (if products available, set up taste panel)
   - ease of use (equipment, preparation, additions needed?)
   - preparation time (based on knowledge of types of soup, or practical experiment).

   Use the information from the comparison to compile the survey.
   - Ask a variety of questions ensuring that you have a mix of open and closed questions.
   - Write out approximately ten questions allowing room to insert the answers.
   - Display your results using a computer if available.
   - Bar charts and pie charts are useful for visual display of information.

Activities page 47

1. **At what temperature should: a) chilled food; b) frozen food be stored in a supermarket?**

   a) between -1°C and 8°C, but preferably below 4°C, due to risk of listeria infection

   b) between -18°C and -29°C.

2. **Where would you be likely to find the following products in your supermarket?**

   See Table 4.

Table 4	
Chilled cabinet	**Freezer**
pork sausages	vegetarian burgers
vegetarian burgers	corn on the cob
coleslaw	blackberry sorbet
tofu	pizza
pizza	

3. **How can Bestco make sure that they do not have to throw away food at the end of the day?**

   Suggestions might include:
   - chilled cabinet placed prominently near entrance to attract lunchtime shoppers
   - emphasise freshness of products with signs, e.g. 'freshly made'
   - market research to find out what is required and therefore avoid wastage
   - produce small quantities of each type of sandwich at first
   - monitor sales to respond to demand for particular products
   - reduce price of products towards end of day to avoid leftover stock at closing time.

Activities page 49

1. a) **Advantages of irradiation as a method of preservation?**

   Suggestions might include:
   - bacteria is killed without the food being affected in terms of taste or appearance
   - stops sprouting and ripening
   - kills pests
   - increases shelf life
   - makes it easier to transport food long distances.

   b) **Why may public be concerned about irradiation?**

Suggested answers   unit 10

Suggestions might include:
- no way of telling if the food as been irradiated
- unfit food may be irradiated and then passed on for sale
- little known about the loss of nutrients in irradiated food
- little known about health effects of eating irradiated food.

c) Would you buy irradiated foods?
Students could tabulate answers in grid format or use a computer to display results in a bar or pie graph.

2. Compare cook-chill and sous-vide.
See Table 5.

Table 5

	Cook-chill	Sous-vide
food preparation	food is prepared in the normal way	food is prepared on sulphurised paper
cooking	food is cooked in the normal way	food is slowly cooked at temperatures between 70°C and 100°C
chilling	blast chilling	blast or water chilling
storage	food is stored at a temperature of of 0-3°C	food is stored at 1-4°C
reheating	reheated to 70-75°C in centre for at least 2 minutes	reheated to 70-75°C in centre for at least 2 minutes

unit 11 Additives

Suggested answers

Activities page 50

1. Which additives are concerned with food preservation and which are concerned with improving the colour and flavour of food?
Food preservation - preservatives and antioxidants
Improving the colour and flavour of food - colours, emulsifiers, flavourings.

2. Match the type of additive with its function:
See Table 6.

Table 6	
preservatives	help keep food longer
colours	improve appearance of food
emulsifiers	help fats and water to mix
flavourings	improve the taste of food
antioxidants	stop fats going rancid

3. Why might people be concerned about additives?
Some people might be concerned about the possible link between additives and allergies, hyperactivity in children and asthma attacks.

4. a) Name three additives in strawberry flavour dessert mix.
Suggestions might include:
- Modified starch - thickener
- Propylene Glycol Monostearate - emulsifier
- Lecithin - emulsifier
- Disodium Monophosphate - gelling agent
- Sodium Pyrophosphate - gelling agent
- Flavourings - do not need to be individually listed
- Carmine - colour
- Annatto - colour.

b) Explain functions of each additive.
Suggestions might include:
- gelling agent controls texture
- emulsifier controls texture
- colour adds aesthetic appeal.

c) Why list additives?
Suggestions might include:
- it is a legal requirement
- consumers have a right to know
- consumer might have an allergy to a particular additive and wish to avoid it.

Case Study
Food labelling

Activities page 52

1. a) RNI for riboflavin for boys 11-14.
1.2 mg per day.

b) Percentage of this provided by bran cereal and milk.
50%.

2. Amount of cereal needed to meet 25 year old man's RNI for riboflavin.
100g cereal.

3. a) According to packet, how much B12 needed daily?
1µg.

100g of cereal provides 0.85µg vitamin B12.
This is 85% of RDA.
Therefore 1.0µg is 100% of RDA.

b) Is this enough for most people?
The RNI for vitamin B12 for people over 15 is 1.50µg. The Recommended Daily Amount which is suggested on the cereal packet is 1.0µg. This would be sufficient to meet the needs of most children up to the age of 10 years, but may not be enough for people older than this.

NB In second and subsequent printings of the students' book questions 3a and 3b will be replaced by:

3. Is bran cereal a useful source of vitamin B12? Justify your answer.
Bran cereal is a useful source of vitamin B12. The cereal packet states that a bowl of bran cereal and milk provides 0.75 µg

20

Suggested answers — Unit 11

B12, which is 75% of the RDA. However, the information on the cereal packet is based on the RDA rather than the RNI. The RNI for B12 for people over 15 years is 1.50μg, so a bowl of bran cereal and milk only provides 50% of the daily needs for most people in this group. This is still a useful contribution to the diet.

4. Percentage of RNI for iron supplied by bowl of cereal:
30 year old man - 41% of the RNI is provided
30 year old woman - 24% of the RNI is provided
3 year old girl - 52% of the RNI is provided
(figures given to nearest whole number)

The method used to answer this question is:

$$\frac{\text{Amount of iron}}{\text{RNI}} \times 100 = \% \text{ RNI supplied}$$

e.g.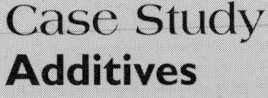

Case Study: Additives

Activities page 53

1. Why buy sulphured apricots?
They have a better colour and a longer shelf life.

2. Points for discussion about use of sulphites.
- Do food manufacturers have a responsibility to the consumer?
- Is the risk of consumer reaction to sulphites too small to be taken notice of by manufacturers?
- What action could be taken by the manufacturer?
- Are warnings appropriate? if so what form should they take?
- Interested parties could be the environmental health department (see Unit 30), television consumer programmes, food manufacturers, supermarkets.

3. List products containing sulphites.
This activity may be set as homework, with discussion to follow in a later lesson.

Case Study: Extended life milk

Activities page 53

1. Students are asked to carry out a taste test on milk.
These are some points to consider:
- see Unit 23 for more information on taste panels
- use coded samples (i.e. identical containers marked A, B, C, etc.)
- check volunteers for allergies.

2. Advantages and disadvantages of different milks.
Suggestions might include:
Fresh milk
ADVANTAGES: familiar flavour.
DISADVANTAGES: needs refrigeration, short shelf life.
UHT
ADVANTAGES: very long shelf life, no specialised storage required until opened, convenient portions available.
DISADVANTAGES: lower vitamin content than fresh milk, some people dislike the flavour.
Extended life milk
ADVANTAGES: long shelf life, good flavour, convenient portions available, higher vitamin content than UHT milk.
DISADVANTAGES: lower vitamin content than fresh milk, needs refrigeration.

3. Suggestions for testing consumer reactions:
- taste panels using volunteers on the ground
- trial usage on identified flights
- involving airline passengers in comparative tests whilst on their journeys
- different types of test could include: rating, hedonic scale, triangle, ranking and open evaluation.

NB: Reactions to flavours alter when flying so trials should be carried out both in the air and on the ground.

4. Suggestions for other marketing opportunities for extended life milk might include:
- restaurants and cafés
- mass catering, e.g. hospitals, school canteens
- long distance transport, e.g. Eurostar, Orient Express, coach
- camping (convenient packaging but must be consumed rapidly).

Healthy eating

Suggested answers

Activities page 54

1. Suggest three possible changes that you could make to improve your diet.
Students should make their answer relevant to their own diet.
Suggestions might be:
- reduce the amount of fat, particularly saturated fat (e.g. cook food by grilling, baking or steaming rather than deep or shallow frying)
- reduce the amount of sugar (if necessary replacing with calories from a carbohydrate source)
- limit sugary treats such as cakes and biscuits to one portion per day
- reduce the amount of salt (e.g. by not adding salt when cooking vegetables).

2. What are dietary targets and why are they set by the government?
Dietary targets are long term nutritional goals. These goals apply to all the people in Britain. They are set by the government because, if the targets are met, the health of the nation would be improved.

3. How do suggestions in article meet with dietary targets?
Some recommendations seem helpful, supporting guidelines for a healthy diet, while others seem unhelpful, appearing to contradict them:

HELPFUL
- recommends vegetables (good source of starch, NSP, vitamins and minerals)
- recommends yogurt (if unsweetened, low fat variety this is a good source of protein and calcium)
- recommends unsweetened drinks
- allows limited amounts of alcohol (though why at the end of the meal is a mystery!)

UNHELPFUL
- tells you not to eat bread (but this is an excellent energy food which contains little or no fat)
- recommends cheese (but some kinds contain a very high proportion of saturated fat).

Activities page 55

1. Advise Javed on his choice of food.
Suggestions might include:
- eat fewer chips but more potatoes - e.g. jacket potatoes, new potatoes with skins
- grill or steam food rather than frying
- eat more starchy foods that keep you feeling fuller for longer - these are better than foods containing sugar energy
- eat fruit and vegetables rather than crisps and sweets
- eat regularly and in small amounts
- always have breakfast.

2. a) Compare fats for frying chips.
The most expensive is olive oil but it does contains the lowest amount of monounsaturated fat. The cheapest is lard which contains the highest amount of saturated fat and the lowest amount of polyunsaturated fat.

b) Which fat would you use?
Olive oil is not a good choice for deep frying as it is expensive and tends to cling to food making it very greasy. In terms of health, lard is a poor choice of fat. A better choice for frying chips would be a vegetable oil which is low in saturates and high in monounsaturates or polyunsaturates, e.g. rapeseed or sunflower oil.

Activities page 56

1. Improving the NSP content in pizza.
Suggestions might include:
- use wholemeal flour for the base
- use variety of vegetables such as sweetcorn, beans, peppers.

2. State five different desserts containing natural sugars.
Suggestions might include:
- fresh fruit salads using fresh orange or apple juice
- dried dates, figs, apricots
- natural yogurts sweetened with fruit juice or purée
- pies and tartlets using fruit in natural juice
- flapjacks or cereal bars sweetened with dried fruit.

Suggested answers

unit 12

3. Design a packed lunch for a walker.
Students should consider the following points:
- include high calorie foods to replace energy used up by the walker
- easy to transport (food that will not easily squash or break)
- food should not need refrigeration
- should contain some moist foods
- include fibre in the form or fruit, flapjacks or wholemeal bread

Example: one or two varieties of sandwiches or rolls, moist cake such as fruit cake, flapjacks or loaf cake, fresh fruit and juice.

4. a) Comparison of lunches eaten by three students.
- Decide upon the portion sizes to be included.
- Use food tables to complete a comparison chart.

b) Suggest two ways to improve diet.
Suggestions might include:
- Kerry - replace the fizzy orange drink with unsweetened orange juice, eat jacket potato instead of chips
- Gurrinder - replace the can of cola with fruit juice, substitute cheese for jam in sandwich
- Peter - replace white bread with wholemeal bread, add more fibre, e.g. a slice of low fat carrot cake.

Activities page 57

1. Trigger suggestions about sugar in diet:
- drinks (in product and added at table)
- confectionery
- biscuits, cakes, pies and puddings
- cereals (in product and added at the table)
- sauces and pickles
- tinned vegetables
- added to cream, fruit or yogurt
- ice cream and lollies.

2. Low salt snack foods for a children's party.
Suggestions might include:
- egg mayonnaise sandwiches
- home made chicken nuggets
- low salt cheese spread piped onto celery sticks
- fruit kebabs
- vegetable and low salt cheese kebabs.

3. Why do alcoholic fruit drinks appeal to young people?
Suggestions might include:
- sweet flavour masks strong alcohol taste
- colour of the drink is not usually connected with alcohol - more like a child's drink
- fruity flavours suggest a non-alcoholic drink
- packaging designed to appeal to young people.

unit 13 Illness and disorders

Suggested answers

Activities page 58

1. Possible causes of anorexia nervosa.
Appearance is important to groups highlighted in question. Keeping a trim figure in order to succeed as an athlete or as a model could trigger food phobia.

2. Devise a day's menu for boy with Prader Willi syndrome.

Breakfast cereal or porridge
fresh fruit juice
scrambled eggs on toast with tomato

Mid morning apple

Lunch spaghetti bolognese
green salad
banana custard

Dinner jacket potato
baked beans
coleslaw
lemon meringue pie

or any reasonable suggestions.

Strategies to help Jay could include:
- stick to the meals he has planned
- high fibre diet will help to give a sense of fullness
- stay away from other people when they are snacking
- carry sugar free chewing gum
- ensure work colleagues know about eating problem.

Activities page 59

1. Plan a menu for group including coeliac.
For example:
- vegetable soup
- chicken casserole with a selection of fresh vegetables
- creamy rice pudding

or any reasonable suggestions.

2. a) Which soft drinks harmful to teeth?
Suggestions might include:
- fizzy drinks
- low calorie drinks (contain citric acid)
- sweetened squashes
- sweetened tea and coffee
- sweetened milk drinks.

b) Which drinks better for dental health?
Suggestions might include:
- water (still or sparkling)
- milk
- unsweetened tea, coffee or milk drinks (or use artificial sweetener).

c) Ways of reducing damage to teeth.
Suggestions might include:
- drink cola all at once
- do not sip from one drink for a long time
- drink cola with a meal
- clean teeth after meals or chew sugar free gum for a few minutes to clean mouth.

Case Study
Tesco's Healthy Eating campaign

Activities page 60

1. Suggest questions for nutrition advice service.
Any reasonable answer acceptable.

2. Advantages of Tesco Healthy Eating products.
Suggestions might include:
- products are low in fat and/or
- high in fibre and/or
- have the right balance of sugar and salt
- low fat/sugar products may help consumers to lose weight
- low fat products may help consumers to reduce cholesterol levels
- product range may help consumers to meet healthy eating guidelines
- product range may help consumers take step towards healthier lifestyle.

Suggested answers unit 13

3. Which spread better as part of healthy eating plan?
- The spread with the pink label is lower in fat, sodium and energy content.
- It also has a higher proportion of monounsaturated/polyunsaturated fat to saturated fat.

4. a) Why buy Healthy Eating Cod Fillets?
Suggestions might include:
- white fish is low in fat
- coating has less than one third of the fat of a standard breaded fish
- product is 'nutritionally balanced and provides the right proportion of fat, sugars and salt as recommended by leading nutritional experts' - as long as the rest of the meal does not upset this balance.

4. b) Suggest meal including Cod Fillets.
Any reasonable suggestions, for example:
- serving suggestion as shown on Figure 2
- salad and low fat chips.

Case Study
Parkwood House day nursery

Activities page 61

1. a) Suggest changes to recipes to adapt for dairy free diet.
Suggestions might include:
Macaroni cheese
- soya milk made into Béchamel sauce
- Béchamel sauce with puréed tomatoes or mushrooms added
- any other flavouring which would be acceptable to small children.

Bread and butter pudding
- soya milk and vegetable margarine instead of milk and butter
- could add sultanas, marmalade or other flavouring.

b) Alternative protein foods for dairy free diet.
Meat (but not at Parkwood House); fish; eggs; soya, tofu and TVP products; peas, beans and lentils; cereals; freshly sprouted beans and seeds.

c) Plan day's food for dairy free diet.
Any reasonable suggestions, for example:
Morning snack   cream crackers with yeast extract.
Lunch   vegetable crumble, mushroom sauce
                 bread and butter pudding (adapted)
High tea   sardine sandwiches, crumpets.

3. a) Suggest changes to recipes to adapt for gluten free diet.
Suggestions might include:
Cheese and tomato sandwiches
- rice crackers with cheese and tomato.

Tuna and sweetcorn quiche
- pastry made with rice flour or specially prepared flour for coeliacs
- base made from grated potato
- filling topped with mashed potato.

b) What other foods contain gluten?
Suggestions might include:
- breads
- cakes
- biscuits
- pasta
- sausages bound with breadcrumbs
- batters, sauces, some soups (may contain flour)
- most breakfast cereals.

c) Plan day's food for gluten free diet.
Any reasonable suggestions, for example:
Morning snack   oat crackers with cheese spread

Lunch   lentil shepherd's pie, fresh vegetables
                 rice pudding, fruit sauce

High tea   rice crackers with egg and cress
                 fresh fruit

4. a) Plan a week's menus for Parkwood House.
For a shorter activity, or for less able students, weekly menus can be based on the sample menu on the page. Modifications can be suggested for special needs groups. For a more extended activity or for more able students, a new weekly menu can be developed.

b) Write a shopping list for the week and estimate total cost.
Once the menu in a) has been approved, students could complete this shopping list as homework. The list should include all the main ingredients required for the recipes. Costing should be based on prices at time of lesson.

c) Keeping food bill down
Suggestions might include:
- buy foods which are in season and therefore cheaper
- where practical buy in bulk
- make good use of low cost, high protein ingredients, such as pulses
- prepare home made dishes rather than expensive ready prepared meals
- use ready prepared components, such as frozen pastry, sparingly
- make recipes in bulk and freeze excess for another day, or to sell as 'take away' meals.

unit 14 Food materials

Suggested answers

Activities page 62

1. Components of pizza.
Flour, salt, yeast, water, cheese, tomatoes, other flavouring ingredients.

2. Ingredients which have undergone primary processing.
- flour - milling
- fresh vegetables - washing
- herbs - drying.

3. Ingredients which have undergone secondary processing.
- Milk made into cheese
- tomatoes canned or puréed
- other flavouring ingredients, e.g. curing and/or smoking of bacon and ham.

Activities page 63

1. Reasons why catering trade uses pre-manufactured food components.
Suggestions might include:
- guaranteed quality
- consistent results
- saves time
- little or no skill required to use them
- some have a relatively long shelf life
- can be used as part of more complex dishes
- waste is minimised
- flavour, colour and appearance can be guaranteed - it is therefore a means of quality control
- costs can be predicted accurately.

2. a) Investigate stock products.
Students could consider the following points:
- product suitable for vegetarians?
- shelf life and storage requirements
- cost and value for money
- salt content and nutritional implications.

b) Suggest dishes made with different types of stock.
Students should be able to refer to cookery books.
Suggestions might include:
- soups
- stews
- casseroles
- pasta dishes.

c) Advantages of using ready made stock.
Suggestions might include:
- saves time
- could save money depending on type of stock bought
- flavour variation is possible according to personal preferences
- proportion of ingredients can be controlled according to taste and nutritional requirements
- can make use of foods readily available at home
- can freeze excess in convenient portions.

unit 15

Measurement and proportion

Activities page 64

1. How were manufacturers and retailers affected by 'metrication day'?
From 1 October 95 it became illegal to sell prepacked foods in pounds and ounces rather than kilos and grams. Manufacturers and retailers had to take measures to comply with this new law.
Suggestions might include:
- ensure that weighing equipment operated in metric measurements
- ensure that labelling equipment printed the new metric measurements
- train staff to understand the new measurements
- explain the change to their customers.

2. Why were some people concerned about changeover?
Some consumers felt that prices would rise. There is some justification for this as the conversion costs were high. Sainsbury spent in excess of £1 million on producing conversion charts for distribution in their stores. The National Association of Shopkeepers admitted that new weighing equipment had to be paid for, and the only way was to increase prices.

3. Convert shopping list from imperial into metric measurement.

½lb cheddar cheese	= 200g
1lb carrots	= 500g
5lb potatoes	= 2.5kg
4oz wine gums.	= 100g
1pt milk	= 568ml/500ml

Activities page 65

1. Why does McCain portion look bigger?
The cut is different. The chips are longer, therefore take up more room in the receptacle, leaving more space between each chip.

2. Why would retailer get 'more portions per pound'?
A portion of chips is usually measured by volume, not weight. Because McCain chips are longer, fewer need to be given in each portion. This would mean that the restaurant would get 'more portions per pound'.

3. Which chips would a restaurant manager choose?
McCain chips would offer a higher income per kilo of chips. However, they may cost a lot more than another brand. A fast food restaurant manager would need to consider the cost of McCain French Fries compared to alternative varieties to decide if the advantage offered by the longer cut would increase overall income.

Activities page 67

1. Compare samples of pastry cooked by different methods.
Answers will depend on the degree of skills acquired.
- Flavour - should not vary much.
- Texture - might range from short and crisp to hard and rubbery.
- Ease of preparation - by hand gives least washing up; food processor may be faster but gives more washing up.

2. Suggest dishes using paté sucré and filo pastry:
Paté sucré French patisserie e.g. strawberry tarts, apple flans.
Filo pastry mince pies, apple strudel.

3. Suggest ingredients to add to shortbread:
- chocolate chips
- cocoa
- glacé cherries
- nuts
- peanut butter
- spices, e.g. mixed spice, cloves, ginger.

4. Compare samples of cheese sauce.
This will be a subjective answer. Roux is the traditional method but slow. The all in one method needs a lot of attention in the early stages. The packet mix is the best for those who have difficulty making sauces.

unit 15
Suggested answers

5. Which pastry is used for these dishes?

pork pie = hot water crust pastry
éclairs = choux pastry
apple pie = sweet short crust pastry.

Case Study
Bramley's Coffee House

Activities page 68

1. What products from storecupboard could be used in recipes?
- sticky toffee pudding and custard - ready made custard, sponge layers
- tuna and bean salad - canned tuna, canned kidney beans
- vegetable lasagne - lasagne verde, garlic purée, salt
- beef and chestnut casserole - beef bouillon mix, canned chestnuts, salt
- tiramisu - ready made custard, sponge layers
- tomato and basil soup - vegetable bouillon mix, canned tomatoes, salt, pepper
- fruit and nut flap jacks - chopped mixed nuts, sultanas, desiccated coconut.

2. Investigate three products from storecupboard.
Any reasonable answer.

3. Advantages and disadvantages of standard components.
Suggestions might include:
ADVANTAGES
- consistency of result, in appearance, size and flavour
- tinned, packaged and dried goods easier to store in limited space
- cost of food unlikely to vary much over year
- little waste.

DISADVANTAGES
- fresh goods in season may be cheaper than canned or dried
- flavour may be poorer than fresh equivalent.

4. a) Which products should be bought daily?
Suggestions might include:
- fresh milk
- cream
- bread/baguettes
- fresh gateâux.

b) How could Bramleys avoid waste of fresh produce?
Suggestions might include:
- keep perishable goods to minimum
- ensure all perishable goods are stored correctly, e.g. potatoes stored well ventilated and in dark to prevent greening.

5. How should stock rotation be organised?
See p.117 of students' book for an explanation of how stocks should be rotated. Stock rotation at Safeway stores is explained on p.45. The picture on p.137 shows how a catering business monitors the rotation of stock in its freezer.

Case Study
Measurement at British Bakeries

Activities page 69

1. Why should breadmaking process be the same in each site?
Loaves of Nimble, Hovis and Mothers Pride must be the same no matter what part of the country they come from. The customer expects consistent quality.

2. Name a stage where measurement by following takes place.

weight — mixing 1 (flour, water), mixing 2 (salt, improvers) and dividing (dough)
volume — mixing 1 (yeast, vinegar)
height — checking height.

3. What might happen if too much of following ingredients were used?

yeast — too much gassing (suitable only for Nimble or Danish breads, where a lighter texture is required)
flour — tight dough which may not rise properly, resulting in a reduced volume
salt — reduced volume, flavour is affected.

4. Average finished bread weight is low.
a) How could bakery remedy problem?
Suggestions might include:
- check weighing of flour and water in mixing 1 stage and increase if necessary
- check weighing of the raw dough portions in dividing stage and increase if necessary.

b) Which part of process is affected?
Mixing 1 and dividing.

c) What changes need to be made?
- Check for human error.
- Check computerised scales for faults.
- Service any machinery which is faulty.
- Increase weights of basic ingredients or raw dough portions if necessary.

unit 16 Adapting recipes

Activities page 70

1. Adapt recipe for limited budget.
Suggestions might include:
- reduce amount of meat and increase vegetable content
- substitute water for wine
- substitute margarine for butter.

2. Adapt recipe for vegetarian.
The minced lamb and dripping must be replaced with suitable alternatives.
Suggestions might include:
- substitute TVP for meat
- use a variety of vegetables, possibly with a proportion of chopped nuts
- include a proportion of pulses with the vegetables
- substitute dripping with vegetable fat or oil.

In addition, some vegetarians may prefer not to eat butter or milk, in which case vegetable spreads and soya milk may be used.

3. Adapt recipe for child.
Suggestions might include:
- prepare small individual portions
- decorate top with tomato slices, peas and cooked carrot rings to make a face or the child's name.

4. Reduce fat content of recipe.
Suggestions might include:
- use lean meat
- omit dripping or use low fat alternatives
- use skimmed milk or low fat yogurt in the mashed potato.

5. Add colour to dish.
Suggestions might include:
- add sweetcorn, or sliced red and green peppers to the meat
- add a little tomato purée to the mashed potato
- add grated cheese to the top of the potato and grill until golden
- garnish with tomato and parsley.

6. Effect of changes made.
Students could design a table like the one below to help them organise their answer to this question.

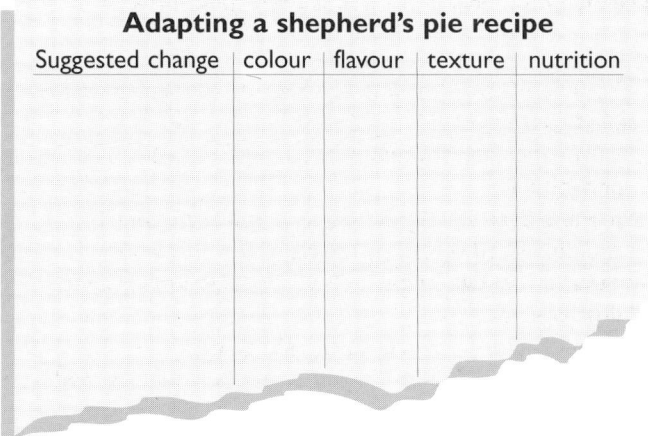

Adapting a shepherd's pie recipe

Suggested change	colour	flavour	texture	nutrition

Activities page 71

1. Which components affect:

a) texture?
Affected by the choice of the basic ingredient, e.g. a chicken burger made with minced meat will have a finer texture than a vegetable burger; a fish burger will have a flaky texture and some beef burgers can be quite rubbery. The coating also affects texture, for example, breadcrumbs give a crispy surface.

b) flavour?
Affected by the choice and proportion of components used and the inclusion of additional flavourings both natural (e.g. onion, garlic) and artificial.

c) nutritional value?
Affected by the proportion of protein, fat, NSP, salt, vitamins, minerals and carbohydrate in the burger components. It is also affected by the chosen cooking method. Cost should also be considered when assessing nutritional content as the cheaper brands are likely to contain more carbohydrate based filler, and possibly meat which contains more fat.

unit 16 — Suggested answers

2. Meats which could be used in burgers:
- lamb
- beef
- chicken
- pork
- turkey
- sausage meat
- venison.

3. Fish which could be used in burgers:
- cod
- haddock
- plaice
- coley
- salmon.

4. Flavouring ingredients which could be used in burgers:
- onions
- garlic
- chilli
- parsley
- mustard
- lemon.

5. Suitable coatings for fish or vegetable burger:
- egg and breadcrumbs
- seasoned flour
- crushed crisps
- crushed stuffing mix
- finely chopped nuts
- sesame seeds.

6. Why might non-vegetarian choose Quorn burger?
Suggestions might include:
- a low fat alternative to meat
- a high fibre alternative to meat
- adds variety to the diet.

7. Draw up specification for economy burger.
In addition to the points given on the page you could ask students to consider the target group and possible price range for the product. See Unit 22 for more information on drawing up a specification.

unit 17
Cooking food

Activities page 72

1. What is this product?
A frozen beefburger.

2. Which is quickest method of cooking?
Grilling. Other methods suggested would take much longer to prepare before cooking.

3. What kind of heat transference takes place with each method?
grill - radiation and conduction
bake - convection and conduction
barbecue - radiation and conduction.

Activities page 73

1. Which cooking methods best for low fat diet?
Boiling, poaching, grilling and baking.

2. What are benefits and costs of different cooking methods?
See Table 6.

3. A class discussion should help to generate ideas before students begin this assignment.

Activities page 75

1. Suggest cooking methods for:
a) pizza - baking
b) lasagne - baking
c) fish cakes - grilling
d) broccoli - steaming.

2. Identify cooking method which matches statement:
a) fast/food browns - grilling
b) water/food does not touch it - steaming
c) loss of water soluble vitamins - boiling
d) browning/flavour development - roasting.

Table 6		
Cooking method	**Benefits**	**Costs**
microwave cookery	fast, cheaper to run than a conventional oven	food may suffer from a loss in flavour and/or texture
moist methods of cooking	foods absorb flavours of cooking liquid tougher foods can be tenderised	vitamin loss is great unless cooking liquid is eaten
stir frying	rapid cooking retains nutrients	preparation time may be longer as food needs to be cut into small pieces needs constant attention
casseroling	as for moist methods can use cheaper cuts of meat	long slow cooking means that power costs may be higher

unit 17 — Suggested answers

Activities page 76

1. What heat transference takes place with wok cookery?
Conduction and convection.

2. Why prepare ingredients in advance?
Food needs to be in very small pieces because it is cooked rapidly. There would not be time to do this once cooking has begun, therefore everything has to be prepared before cooking commences.

3. Suggest ways of preparing ingredients:
Chicken breast - cut into small pieces, possibly marinated for extra flavour.
Reason - meat needs to be cooked thoroughly and quickly. Insufficiently cooked chicken could result in food poisoning.

Mange tout - wash and dry thoroughly.
Reason - wash to remove pesticides etc. Dry to prevent spitting in the wok.

Carrots - wash and/or peel and cut into sticks.
Reason - carrots are a root vegetable and should always be washed. Older carrots should be peeled. New carrots can be just be scrubbed. There is a school of thought which believes that all carrots should be peeled because of the chemicals used in production.

Activities page 77

1. Why is it important to cook food thoroughly in a microwave?
Insufficient cooking can result in harmful bacteria being present, which may cause food poisoning.

2. Why do consumers need to know power output and heating category?
With this information, the consumer can confidently use the equipment to heat or cook commercially pre-prepared dishes. The instructions on product packaging give timings according to the power output or heating category of a microwave.

3. What might happen if fish pie cooked for:
a) 6 mins in 650W oven = underdone
b) 6 mins in 800W oven = overdone
c) 4 mins in 750W oven = underdone.

unit 18
Mixing, cutting, forming and shaping

Activities page 78

Complete table showing manipulative processes and tools
Table 7 shows some suggestions.

Table 7

DISH	MIXING PROCESS	CUTTING PROCESS	FORMING/ SHAPING PROCESS
Butterfly cakes	Creaming mixture: electric mixer	Cutting out top of cake: paring knife	1. Baking cakes: bun tin 2. Filling with butter cream: piping bag and nozzle
Meringues	Beating egg white: electric mixer		Piping: piping bag and nozzle
Pizza	Mixing bread dough: by hand	Cutting and dicing filling: sharp knife	Shaping the bread dough: rolling pin
Cheesecake	Whisking and mixing filling: hand whisk	1. Crushing biscuits: food processor 2. Lemon rind: zester 3. Lemon juice: lemon squeezer	1. Shaping cake: in tin or flan dish 2. Piping cream: piping bag and nozzle
Cream of tomato soup		1. Cutting vegetables: vegetable knife 2. Blending soup: food processor	
Trifle	1. Making custard: wooden spoon 2. Making jelly: metal spoon	1. Cutting sponges: knife 2. Cutting fruit: paring knife	1. Shaping trifle: shaped dishes 2. Piping cream: piping bag and nozzle
Chicken vol-au-vents	1. Making pastry: by hand 2. Making sauce: wooden spoon	1. Dicing chicken: sharp knife 2. Cutting pastry: plain or fluted cutters	Filling: piping bag or spoon
Scones	1. Making dough: rubbing in by hand 2. Mixing liquid: metal spoon	Cutting scones: plain or fluted cutters	Adding filling: piping cream or spreading jam
Jam tarts	Making pastry: by hand	Cutting pastry: plain or fluted cutters	Adding filling: teaspoon

unit 18 — Suggested answers

Activities page 79

1. List of rules which you would display beside industrial slicer.
Suggestions might include:
- never use this machine unless trained to do so
- never use this machine without authorisation
- always follow the correct procedure when using this machine
- never leave the machine with the guard removed
- never leave the machine with motor running
- ensure the machine is dismantled correctly
- never leave the blades submerged in water
- ensure that the machine is serviced regularly.

2. Why is industrial equipment composed largely of stainless steel?
Suggestions might include:
- does not corrode or rust
- can be sanitised
- dishwasher proof
- can withstand heavy duty wear.

3. Why are industrial machines operated by push buttons?
Suggestions might include:
- machine can be easily turned off in the case of an emergency
- can be operated using back of hand or arm thus avoiding risk of cross-contamination.

4. Explain the need for an emergency cut-off button.
In the event of an accident, e.g. hands or clothing being trapped in the machinery, the equipment can be immediately turned off.

5. Why more emphasis on aesthetic appeal of domestic equipment?
Suggestions might include:
- electrical equipment is 'on display' in a domestic kitchen
- people want a colour coordinated kitchen
- people want 'white goods' which are compact and attractive to look at

Activities page 80

1. Functions of a domestic food processor.
Suggestions might include:
- mixing
- cutting
- chopping
- shredding
- grating
- mincing
- liquidising
- dough making
- blending
- slicing
- puréeing
- chipping
- whisking.

2. Advantages and disadvantages of using a food processor?
Suggestions might include:
ADVANTAGES
- compact
- versatile
- cheaper than a food mixer with separate attachments
- easy to use
- easy to clean
- easy to maintain.

DISADVANTAGES
- can only mix limited amounts of food at any one time
- unsuitable for very small quantities of food
- need to clean all parts of machine even if only used for one function.

3. Design a menu using functions of a food processor.
Any reasonable answer, for example:

liver paté	blending and liquidising
stuffed turkey	making bread crumbs and stuffings
	mixing bread sauce
Christmas pudding	mixing pudding

Activities page 81

1. Outlets which might use automatic potato peeler.
Suggestions might include:
- fish and chip shop
- fast food burger bar
- steakhouse.

2. Items useful to a public house.
Suggestions might include:
- automatic potato peeler - saves time when making chips
- sandwich toaster - gives professional finish to lunchtime snacks
- slicer - slicing whole meats such as ham, beef and turkey
- food processor - multi-purpose machine, useful for pastries, fillings, stuffing, desserts such as cheesecakes and mousses.

3. Justify the purchase of industrial machines
Suggestions might include:
- larger capacity for catering size proportions
- motors are designed for prolonged use and are larger and more powerful
- good safety design features sometimes at the expense of aesthetic design, e.g. cut off switch
- service contracts available.

4. Small butcher's shop making sausages would require:
- food processor
- sausage making machine.

unit 19
Using tools safely

Activities page 83

1. Equipment evaluation.
Example - food processor should:
- have firmly secured nuts and bolts with none of the mechanism easily accessible
- have no cracks or crevices
- be durable and hard wearing
- be easy to disassemble
- be easy to sanitise and clean all separate parts
- be made of plastic or stainless steel
- bowl should not scratch easily or it would trap bacteria
- be dishwasher-proof.

2. a) Why should a metal mitten be worn?
To avoid serious damage to the fingers, hand or arm due to the force and pressure applied when jointing meat, which could cause permanent injury in the event of an accident.

b) Why is it good safety practice to keep knives sharpened?
If knives are kept sharp they will easily slice through food, in particular meat, fruit and vegetables. If allowed to go blunt when pressure is applied the knife could slip, resulting in accidents and injury.

c) What to remember when cleaning knives?
Suggestions might include:
- never leave in water - another person could unknowingly put their hands into the water and cut themselves
- use bacterial wipes and sanitiser to prevent bacterial growth
- clean knives immediately after use
- clean knives with blade facing away from you.

3. a) What is the purpose of colour coded catering equipment?
Colour coding is used to prevent cross-contamination. It ensures that knives or other equipment are only used for specific foods.

b) Design a poster.

4. Hazards and hygiene considerations when preparing pan-fried lamb.
See Table 8.

5. Work experience safety training programme.
Example outline:
Food preparation - growth of bacteria, food hygiene for food handlers (personal hygiene, rules of the kitchen, correct clothing, cross-contamination), food preservation and storage, safe use of equipment.

Cooking - safe use of equipment, time and temperature control, hazards involved in different cooking methods.

Transport - storage of food, temperature control, monitoring of equipment. Hygienic presentation and serving of food.

Table 8

Stage	Hazards	Action
Cutting meat	Care should be taken when jointing meat.	Use clean, sharp meat knives which should be cleaned thoroughly after use.
Frying cutlets	Care should be taken when frying oil to ensure oil is correct temperature, to prevent fat spitting	Do not put hot pan in water. Treat all equipment as bacteria contaminated and clean thoroughly after use.
Adding alcohol	Take care when adding - to prevent pan catching fire on a gas flame.	Cook alcohol dish thoroughly. Carefully pour measured amount of alcohol, taking pan off the heat before doing so.
Serving	Avoid burns by using tongs when removing from pan and arranging on a plate.	Ensure equipment used in preparation is not used in serving food to prevent cross-contamination. Serve food immediately or keep food out of the danger zone (3-63°C) until required.

unit 19 — Suggested answers

Case Study: The Hotwich

Activities page 84

1. a) What happens to sale of sandwiches in winter? Why?
Sales fall by 20% compared to the summer. This could be because in summer, people want a lighter snack and may eat their lunch outside. In winter, when the weather is colder, people may prefer a hot, substantial lunch.

b) Why might people buy a Hotwich in winter?
Suggestions might include:
- offers same ease and convenience of a bought sandwich
- is a hot snack
- is more substantial than a sandwich
- can be heated at home or work.

2. a) What problem did company encounter in designing product?
When heated in a microwave, bread and other baked products become soft and lose texture.

b) What solution did they find?
Green Meadow designed a special packaging sleeve, with a metallic liner, which helps to keep the bread's crusty texture when reheated by microwave.

3. a) What equipment necessary to sell Hotwich?
- Refrigerator - to keep product chilled at 0-4°C.
- Microwave - to heat product quickly.

b) List of instructions.
For example:
- Select Hotwich from refrigerator.
- Remove cardboard sleeve and plastic film.
- Replace sandwich in cardboard sleeve.
- Heat on HIGH for 2 ½ minutes.
- Leave to stand in sleeve for 1-2 minutes, before eating.

TAKE CARE AS CONTAINER AND SANDWICH WILL BE VERY HOT.

Case Study: Dangerous machines

Activities page 84

1. Reasons why accident occurred:
Suggestions might include:
- lack of training
- no safety guard
- poorly maintained equipment.

2. Precautions necessary to prevent future accidents.
Suggestions might include:
- establish a maintenance procedure
- set up a training programme for equipment handlers
- ensure equipment has appropriate guards.

3. Design a safety poster.

Case Study: Making pasta

Activities page 85

1. Properties of durum wheat.
It is a hard grain with a high gluten content.

2. Draw a flow chart of a factory pasta making process.
See Figure 1 for an example.

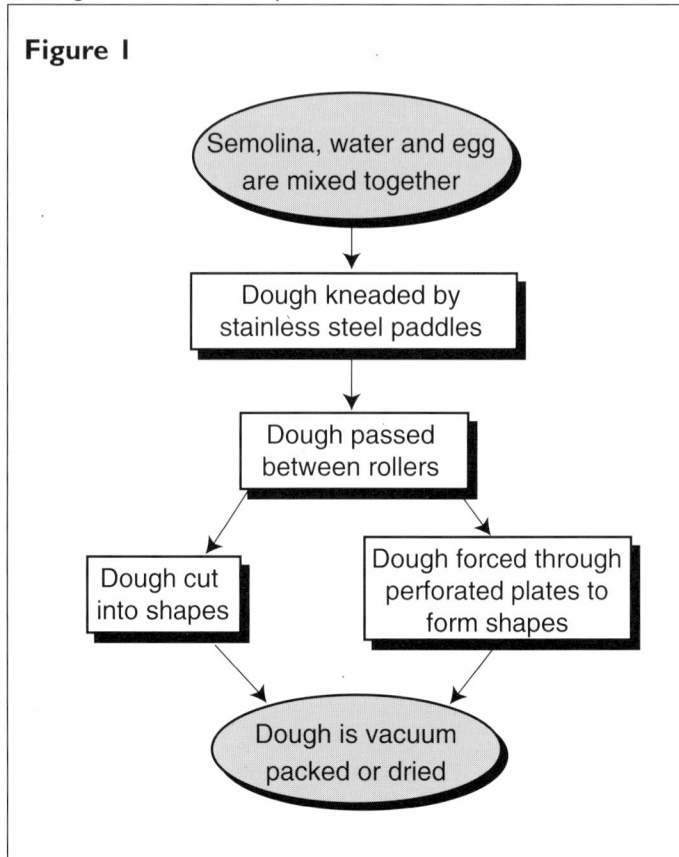

Figure 1

- Semolina, water and egg are mixed together
- ↓
- Dough kneaded by stainless steel paddles
- ↓
- Dough passed between rollers
- ↙ ↘
- Dough cut into shapes | Dough forced through perforated plates to form shapes
- ↘ ↙
- Dough is vacuum packed or dried

Suggested answers

unit 19

3. Compare process of making pasta by hand and in a factory.
See Table 9.

4. a) Why are there so many different shapes of pasta?
Suggestions might include:
- pasta is staple food of Italy - variety of shapes
- variety of shapes complement different flavours and sauces
- some are used for filling; some for accompanying
- different thicknesses and sizes have different cooking times and are therefore used with different dishes.

b) Suggest sauces to go with different shapes.
Suggestions might include:
- spaghetti - bolognese sauce
- macaroni - cheese sauce
- canneloni - seafood sauce.

Table 9

	Hand	Machine
Mixing	eggs are mixed into flour by fork	semolina, water and eggs are mixed by stainless steel paddles
Kneading	takes a long time	stainless steel paddles knead the dough
Rolling	dough is rolled out using a rolling pin	dough is passed through rollers
Cutting/Shaping	cut using a knife or shaped cutters	machines cut shapes or perforated plates form shapes

… # unit 20 Large equipment

Suggested answers

Activities page 86

1. Benefits of an industry standard catering container.
Suggestions might include:
- containers can be used in a wide variety of equipment e.g. ovens, freezers, holding ovens, fridges, chillers etc.
- food can be transferred without the need for excessive handlin e.g. a dish can be frozen, defrosted and cooked in the same container
- all catering equipment is designed to be used with standard size containers.

2. Draw a plan showing size and combination of containers for serving menu.
A variety of answers is possible but the following should be noted:
- large container - main meal, potatoes, dessert
- medium container - vegetables
- small container - gravies and sauces.

Activities page 88

1. Explain how heat cooks an egg using an induction hob.
Heat is only generated within the cooking pan. The hob remains cold, which is why the egg has not cooked directly on the induction hob but has cooked when it has come into contact with the pan.

2. Advantages and disadvantages of an induction hob.
Suggestions might include:
ADVANTAGES
- food will not stick to the hob
- hob is easily cleaned
- temperature is controllable
- hob switches itself off automatically when pan is removed
- uses less power than a conventional hob.

DISADVANTAGES
- hobs are very expensive to buy
- hobs require special cooking pans which are expensive

- will not work using aluminium or copper pans which are magnetic.

3. Catering outlets which would find an induction hob useful.
Suggestions might include:
- back bar units, e.g fast food operations
- small restaurants
- outlets where food is cooked at the customer's table.

4. Match the statements to the types of hobs:
- several pans/flat surface - induction
- fast/easily controlled - gas, halogen, induction
- suits pans with different sized bases - ceramic, halogen
- relies on pans having solid flat bases - radiant disc rings, induction
- produces instant heat - gas, halogen, induction
- is easy to clean - induction, halogen, ceramic.

Activities page 89

1. Suggest appropriate equipment package for each outlet.
riverside restaurant - b
nursing home - c
fish and chip shop - a

2. Which outlet would consider speed of cooking to be a top priority?
Fish and chip shop - customer requires instant service - speed is therefore a top priority.

3. Which outlet would not need a conventional oven?
Fish and chip shop - cooking would take too long.

Activities page 90

1. Operating temperature of a commercial freezer.
-18°C to -29°C

2. Why cool food rapidly before storing in a freezer?

Suggested answers unit 20

To get food from cooked temperature to freezing temperature through the danger zone (3-63°C) quickly thus reducing the risk of bacterial contamination.

3. Advantages of being able to cook-freeze food.
Suggestions might include:
- restaurant can cook and freeze own products reducing costs
- can store own products until required for up to six months
- can make use of foods in season and maintain availability of menu items.

Activities page 91

1. a) What is a flight dishwasher?
A large dishwasher where crockery is loaded onto a conveyor belt fitted with plastic or metal pegs instead of baskets.

b) Two operations where it might be appropriate.
Suggestions might include:
- airline catering
- factory canteen
- large hotel
- prison.

2. Reasons for thermal disinfection rinse:
This rinse ensures that micro-organisms are destroyed. This reduces the risk of cross-contamination and of passing infections to sick people who are particularly vulnerable to infection (the immunocompromised).

3. How does thermal disinfection destroy micro-organisms?
By ensuring that all surfaces reach a temperature of 90°C for 1 second, 80°C for 1 minute or 71°C for 3 minutes. This will remove all harmful organisms.

… # unit 21

Presentation

Suggested answers

Activities page 92

1. Design a Christmas table setting.
Suggestions for approaching the brief:
- Begin with a class discussion about how special occasions are treated in individual families. Record suggestions which are felt to be good or novel.
- Agree a budget.
- Use Christmas magazines to look for illustration ideas.

2. Suggest menu and tableware for summer wedding buffet.
Suggestions for approaching the brief:
- Begin with a class discussion on wedding receptions. Record ideas from students' own experience.
- Use sample menus from local restaurants and hotels which hold wedding receptions.
- Use wedding magazines for illustration ideas.
- Discuss whether the buffet will be self-service or organised with waiting staff.

3. Design colour scheme and china for wholefood café.
Suggestions for approaching the brief:
- Begin with a class discussion about wholefood cafés. Is there one near students' homes or school?
- How might the ethics of the café affect the design (e.g. concern for the environment; interest in healthy eating)?
- Research practical ideas for crockery, etc. For example, pottery could be a good choice in terms of reflecting a wholefood image, but it is expensive to buy and chips easily.

Activities page 93

1. Why serve sauce with poached salmon?
The dish is fairly uninteresting without the sauce, which adds moisture, colour and flavour.

2. Nutritional benefit of using watercress as a garnish.
Watercress contains calcium and Vitamin A. It also contains some iron but it is not easily absorbed from this source.

3. Suggestions for vegetables to accompany this meal might include:
- broccoli
- carrots
- mange tout.

4. Suggestions for desserts with a piped decoration might include:
- trifle
- lemon soufflé
- chocolate mousse.

Case Study
Elro tilting pressure bratt pan

Activities page 94

1. Cooking methods for which bratt pan is suitable.
Braising, frying, boiling, steaming, pressure steaming and pressure stewing.

2. Why does the pan have a wheel on the side?
The wheel activates the mechanism which tilts the pan. This means that large quantities of food or water can be easily removed from the pan. When locked in position, the wheel will hold the pan in an upright or a tilted position.

3. Advantages of steaming process being controlled by a microprocessor.
Suggestions might include:
- the steaming process can be made fully automatic
- food is cooked correctly, without using too much power
- removes 'guesswork'
- leaves staff free to concentrate on other tasks.

4. Design features which help to maintain hygiene standards.
Suggestions might include:
- shallow design and tilting action makes the pan easy to clean
- totally flat base means food will not get stuck in crevices
- rounded corners and simple, smooth, lines make the pan easy to clean

Suggested answers unit 21

- stainless steel finish is hard wearing and, if looked after properly, germ resistant.

5. Reasons for purchasing this piece of equipment.
Suggestions might include:
- versatile
- energy efficient
- latest microprocessor control
- compatible with older pieces of equipment
- could create more room in the kitchen because it does so many tasks
- conserves nutritional content
- retains colour and shape of food
- taste remains good.

Case Study
Heathcotes Brasserie

Activities page 95

1. a) What image is Heathcotes Brasserie trying to present?
Suggestions might include:
- young
- modern
- informal
- clean
- uncluttered.

b) How does environment, table setting and service contribute to this image?
Answers should reflect reasons given in 1. a), for example:
- brightly coloured mural
- bright lighting
- jazz music
- simple, functional table setting
- friendly, chatty staff.

2. Advantages of serving food to customers ready plated.
Suggestions might include:
- portion control is exact, cutting down on waste and costs
- cuts down on serving dishes, therefore initial investment lower
- cuts down on washing up and therefore running costs and storage space needed for this equipment
- saves time spent on serving, leaving waiting staff free to give a more personal service.

3. Meaning of:

Parfait (from French, literally 'perfect')
a) A dessert made from cream, eggs, sugar and flavouring, frozen together.
b) Several layers of different flavoured ice creams, decorated and served in a tall glass.

Terrine (from the name of a small earthenware dish)
Applied to the foods made in this dish, e.g. pâtés, layered savouries, etc.

Ravioli
Small pockets of pasta containing meat, cheese or vegetables. Usually served with a sauce

Pesto (from Italian, literally 'paste')
Italian sauce made by pounding or blending ingredients together. Traditional pesto made from basil leaves, garlic, pine nuts, olive oil and Parmesan cheese. Used as pasta sauce or flavoursome addition to other dishes.

4. Design activity.
You may need to begin with a discussion of exactly what each of these dishes contains.

5. Advise on decor, table settings and menu for a restaurant for young people.
Suggestions for approaching the brief:
- discuss what students would want from a café
- divide class into groups, each working on one aspect of the question
- use design magazines as a resource.

Unit 22: Product development

Suggested answers

Activities page 96

1. What market are Boots aiming at?
Suggestions might include:
- sportsmen/women
- keep fit enthusiasts
- marathon runners
- people who use a great deal of energy and require rapid replenishment of body fluids.

2. How could Boots find out about needs of this market?
Suggestions might include:
- carrying out surveys on people who frequent gyms and leisure centres - continuous survey
- monitoring and recording the use of the product by marathon runners or Olympic squads - quantitative research
- interviewing people who have been given free samples of the product - qualitative research.

3. a) What alternative drinks are available?
This question could be answered in two ways. Firstly, students might suggest the alternatives mentioned in the extract (i.e. water and isotonic drinks). Secondly, they could suggest a whole range of drinks available to all consumers (e.g. sweetened soft drinks, fruit juices, etc). The choice of drink made by a high energy user would depend on whether he or she wanted only to replace:
- lost fluids only (water, low calorie drinks)
- lost fluids and energy (sweetened soft drinks)
- lost fluids, energy and salts (isotonic drinks).

b) How do Boots offer 'added value'?
You could look at how Boots isotonic drinks differ from:
i) ordinary drinks (they are absorbed faster and replace lost fluids, energy and salts)
ii) other isotonic drinks on the market (perhaps Boots are the only company to supply information leaflets giving information relating to the performance of their product).

Activities page 97

1. Name some brands of food products
You could generate information through class discussion or observation/survey in shops.

2. Why does Pepsi need to change its brand image?
To create and/or maintain consumer interest which may attract new customers in the marketing war between Pepsi and Coca-Cola.

3. Would Pepsi's marketing move appeal to costomers aged 16-24? Why?
Students could answer this question on the basis of personal opinion, class discussion or market research within the school to determine how important colour of packaging is to people in the target group. Official data could be collected from food or drink manufacturers on how changes in packaging design affect sales.

4. Conduct a blind testing of Pepsi and Coca-Cola
Unit 23 might help students to carry out this blind tasting.

Activities page 98

1. How might documentary affect sales?
Consumers may demonstrate their dislike of arms trading by refusing to buy products associated with companies which support it.

2. As a consumer, what would you do?
You can generate opinions through class discussion.
Discussion points may include:
- Would you buy a product made by a company involved in arms dealing?
- Would you buy a product which was tested on animals?
- Would you buy a product from a company which paid its workers low wages?
- Would you buy a product from a company which was found to have unhygienic or unsafe working conditions for its employees?
- How do we know where a product comes from and how it is produced?
- Do we have a right to know about workers' rights and conditions?

3. How should manufacturer respond to complaints?
Students could discuss what they think the soft drinks

Suggested answers
unit 22

manufacturer might do in response to customer protest at their involvement with arms dealing, e.g. should they send a letter justifying their position, should they give in to consumer pressure and change their policy, etc.

Activities page 99

1. a) Why are products described as 'functional foods'?
Because the manufacturer claims a specific health benefit in the advertising or product labelling.

b) Who is target market for each product?
Suggestions might include:
- Horlicks - people trying to reduce their intake of fat, e.g. slimmers
- Pact - people concerned about the health of their heart, e.g. people in high risk groups or those with a heart problem
- Toffee Treat - children and groups requiring high energy foods.

c) Why is information given misleading?
The specific health claim means that the product may not be considered as a whole. For example, Toffee Treat and Horlicks have a high sugar content. This may not be immediately recognisable to some consumers, who may focus on the health claims on the label. Pact says that it will help maintain a healthy heart. However, the spread still contains a high proportion of fat. Some of the fat is saturated which is detrimental to the heart.

2. a) Why might slimmers feel that their expectations of the product had not been met?
Suggestions might include:
- advertising may have promoted product as similar to ordinary crisps, but without the fat and calories
- product unlikely to have contained warning as shown in Figure 3
- side effects were unexpected.

b) Why might manufacturer be reluctant to include warning notice?
Suggestions might include:
- insufficient research to prove these side effects occur
- high probability of reduction in sales if warning included.

Activities page 100

1. Brainstorm ideas in response to a brief.
Ideas for carrying out brainstorm:
- use brainstorm charts on pp. 131-2 to help with initial brainstorm
- See Unit 6 for information on nutritional content of food
- see Case Study on p. 61 of students book for ideas on nutritious food for young children
- See Unit 16 for guidance on adapting recipes to meet specific needs.

2. Select one idea to develop.
Consider following points which may help select idea for product development:
- availability and cost of ingredients
- time available
- skill required
- appropriateness of foods
- appropriateness of packaging
- storage requirements
- portioning.

3. Write specification for product.
Ideas to help write specification:
- see Unit 28 for information on production methods
- see Unit 25 for information on packaging the products designed.

Activities page 101

1. Why would a yogurt for babies be profitable for company?
Suggestions might include:
- establishment of a new target group
- convenient and easy to eat food
- nutritious and has healthy image which would appeal to health conscious parents.

2. Describe a market research test that could be carried out.
Suggestions might include:
- discover parents' attitudes to their babies' diets through discussions at clinics - qualitative research
- include a free baby yogurt in a family multi-pack and offer incentives to parents who complete a questionnaire - quantitative research.

3. Design yogurt packaging or TV advert.
Students are offered a choice of design activity. They could work in groups to complete this activity. Ideas to start activity:
- see Unit 25 for what information should be included on packaging
- look at packaging on similar products
- discuss merits of TV advertising
- watch TV adverts to analyse how babies and toddlers can be used to create product appeal.

unit 22 — Suggested answers

> **Case Study**
> **Product development at Birds Eye**

Activities page 102

1. Why collect views of customers?
Manufacturers must respond to consumer requirements so that they have a good idea that the product will sell.

2. Why develop a vegetable based meal product?
Suggestions might include:
- because of health concerns about high fat levels in red meat
- because of increased availability of vegetable products.

3. How did Birds Eye find out which meal idea would appeal to customers?
Birds Eye carried out market research, including:
- using photographs of sample products to judge visual appeal
- asking volunteers to cook samples in their own homes and taste the product.

4. Advantages of testing product in own home.
Suggestions might include:
- product will be cooked under many different conditions
- product will be cooked by people with a variety of skills
- product will be tasted under normal mealtime conditions
- performance of the product will be thoroughly tested
- clarity and accuracy of the cooking instructions may also be checked
- results likely to be more truthful than under artificial testing conditions.

5. Which model of development process:
a) shows how long process takes?
Gantt chart.

b) explains in detail what happens at each stage?
Flow chart.

c) shows how many ideas are narrowed down to one product?
Innovation funnel.

d) How could one of these models help you plan your work?
Students could discuss the advantages and disadvantages of each method. Different models might be useful for planning different aspects of a student's work, for example:
- a Gantt chart might be useful for planning a whole term's work
- a flow chart might be useful for identifying the stages in a design activity
- an innovation funnel might be useful for providing an overview of a work process.

> **Case Study**
> **The wonder bean?**

Activities page 103

Design a new frozen food product using tofu or TVP.
This is a design activity to be undertaken in groups. You may find the following pro formas useful to help students plan:
- p. 133 to help identify tasks, ownership, time scale, etc.
- pp. 131-2 (brainstorm charts) to work through the checklist.

Students may wish to refer to the following Units to help them with particular parts of the checklist:
- Unit 6 - nutritional value of foods
- Unit 8 - dietary needs of different groups
- Unit 17 - use of energy
- Unit 22 - the market, market research, specifications
- Unit 25 - packaging
- Unit 27 - reducing waste (food, energy)
- Unit 28 - production systems
- Unit 29 - quality controls
- Unit 30 - health and safety issues.

You may also find the points relating to Unit 26, activities p. 115, relevant for this activity (these appear on p. 50 of this teachers' guide).

unit 23

Sensory analysis

Activities page 104

1. a) Use sensory descriptors to describe the characteristics of foods.
Students might find it useful to use the pro forma on p. 00.

b) Which sense is easy/difficult to describe?
Students can discuss this question to decide what they think. The order in which senses are generally thought to be easiest to describe is:
- sight
- smell
- taste
- texture.

2. Suggest three dishes with a combination of textures.
Use recipe books to look for foods with several components, e.g. pies and puddings with toppings.

3. Which food aroma do you enjoy most/least?
A class discussion could focus on how liked and disliked aromas may be related to events or feelings, e.g. boiling cabbage and school dinners, chocolate and comfort.

Activities page 105

NB Ratings for the attributes of each product are plotted on the 'legs' of the spider. A higher score is plotted nearer to the word at the end of the leg. For example, Product B is sweeter than Product A.

1. Which product has a more orangey flavour?
Product B.

2. Which product has more bits in it?
Product A.

3. Which product has a more bitter taste?
Product A (though the difference is so small as to be negligible)

4. How to make Product B more like Product A.
Suggestions might include:
- reduce sweetness slightly
- reduce orange flavour
- increase bits in orange to enhance appearance and mouthfeel
- reduce orange colour
- reduce bitter aftertaste.

45

unit 24 Disassembly

Suggested answers

Activities page 106

1. and 2. Sandwich assessment.
Students could either use the comparison pro forma on p. 112 or use the following criteria to create their own:
- size of sandwich
- ratio of bread to filling
- type and amount of spread
- variety of fillings available
- type of packaging
- labelling and design information
- cost.

Activities page 107

1. a) Reasons for public analysts' concerns.
Standards are seen to be falling as the quantity of basic components is being replaced by cheaper and inferior fillers.

b) Products featured in the report:
- potted meats
- breadcrumbed fish products including scampi
- sliced meat
- shaped chicken products
- economy burgers.

2. a) Suggested instructions for disassembly activity as carried out by the *Observer* newspaper:
- defrost Chicken Kiev for one hour
- remove crumb
- examine centre, making notes on the colour, texture and composition of the meat
- stir centre in warm water and note what happens
- record results of stirring in water at five minute intervals, for up to one hour.

b) Why are results of disassembly activity carried out by the newspaper disturbing?
The centre of the Chicken Kiev is not chicken breast as might be expected. Instead it is reconstituted chicken moulded into shape of chicken breast. The product disintegrated when stirred in water, showing that very little muscle meat had been included.

3. Breaded chicken disassembly activity.
Students could use the comparison pro forma on p. 112.

ent
unit 25
Packaging

Activities page 108

1. a) What information must now be included on a sandwich label?
The new Food Labelling Regulations require the following information to be included on sandwich labels:
- name and address of maker
- use by date
- storage instructions
- name of sandwich
- ingredients, including components of ingredients which total more than 25% of the product.

b) Why must this information be included?
Suggestions might include:
- consumer safety (e.g. storage instructions, use by date)
- consumer information (e.g. name of product, ingredients)

2. a) What problems are faced by manufacturers as a result of this requirement?
An increased amount of information needs to be included on a relatively small area on the packaging.

b) How have Breadwinner Foods addressed this problem?
Breadwinner Foods have solved the problem by using transparent labels positioned so that the product can still clearly be seen.

c) Suggest other solutions.
Suggestions might include:
- swing tags
- paper insert inside the sandwich carton
- packaging sandwiches in a single layer rather than stacked as two triangles - this would increase the surface area of the package and therefore give more room for the label.

Activities page 109

1. a) Suggest foods packaged in different materials.
Suggestions might include:
- cans - meat, fish, vegetables, fruit, milk, soft drinks
- glass - fruit juice, pie fillings, milk, sauces
- paper/card - sauces, milk, pies, cereals
- plastic - salads, pasta, meat, fish.

b) Why has manufacturer chosen this material?
Suggestions might include:
- cans - durable, enable long term storage, easily stacked
- glass - product is visible, recyclable, may be traditional and part of corporate image
- paper/card - lightweight, absorbent, recyclable, packages may be standard shapes to facilitate easy stacking
- plastic - efficient protector of fragile foods, hygienic, lightweight.

2. a) List packaging materials for orange juice.
Suggestions might include:
- card cartons
- plastic bottles
- glass bottles
- foil pouch
- frozen in card cylinder.

b) Advantages and disadvantages of each material.
Suggestions might include:
- card cartons -
  ADVANTAGES: easily stacked, allows long term storage, lightweight.
  DISADVANTAGES: may be difficult to open.
- plastic bottles -
  ADVANTAGES: lightweight, product often visible.
  DISADVANTAGES: few recycling facilities, may be difficult to open.
- glass bottles -
  ADVANTAGES: product clearly visible, easily recycled, inexpensive.
  DISADVANTAGES: heavy, fragile.
- foil pouch -
  ADVANTAGES: lightweight, convenient for individual portions.
  DISADVANTAGES: not easily stacked.
- card cylinder -
  ADVANTAGES: compact packaging, useful for concentrates.
  DISADVANTAGES: all product must be defrosted at one time.

unit 25 — Suggested answers

Activities page 110

1. What are special needs of elderly and infirm?
Suggestions might include:
- may have limited mobility
- may have impaired vision and hearing
- may have manipulative problems.

2. List manufacturers' action points for this group.
Suggestions might include:
- market research to find out needs of this group
- reviewing print size on packaging
- developing information in braille
- carrying out tests to find out what form of package closure is preferred by target group.

3. How to reduce, reuse, recycle.
The discussion may include some of the following points.
- What is the difference between reducing, reusing and recycling?
- Who in group does any of these things?
- What is done?
- Comparison of benefits and problems.
- Shopping implications.
- Consideration of local recycling facilities.

4. a) Are food products over packaged?
Students could discuss this question in small groups or as a class, finishing with a class vote.

b) Disadvantages of using several layers of packaging.
Suggestions might include:
DISADVANTAGES:
- increased costs for manufacturer and consumer
- increased weight with implications for transport
- increased use of resources to make packaging
- increased waste which must be transported and disposed of.

You may also wish to consider the advantages.
Suggestions might include:
ADVANTAGES:
- increased product protection
- possible increased hygiene standards.

c) How to inform manufacturers of your opinion.
Suggestions might include:
- write to retailer
- write to manufacturer
- return excess packaging to retailer or manufacturer
- write to consumer programmes on television
- form a pressure group
- boycott products which are over packaged
- contact local Trading Standards Officer and make a formal complaint.

You may wish to ask students at the end of the previous lesson to bring in examples of what they consider over packaged goods, so that the class can analyse these products.

Activities page 111

Make a study of the advertisement of food products on television.
Students should work in groups for this extended research activity. They could use the spider diagram pro forma on p. 00 to establish criteria for advertisement analysis. Ideas could include noting the frequency of advertisements for sweets, breakfast cereals, frozen meals or drinks. Students could look at the time at which advertisements are shown which appeal to children, adults or which have a specific health message.

Case Study
Kelloggs' corn flakes

Activities page 112

1. Why do Kellogg's advertise that they do not make corn flakes for anyone else?
Food manufacturers often supply supermarkets with products which they then sell under their brand name. Kellogg's advertise the fact that they do not do this. There may be several reasons for this.
Suggestions might include that Kellogg's:
- is demonstrating that its corn flakes are a quality product
- wants to emphasise that it is the original manufacturer of corn flakes
- wants to encourage customers to buy only its product
- wants customers to think that its corn flakes are better than the rest.

2. a) Why mimic Kellogg's packaging?
Competitors might believe that by reproducing a similar style of graphics to the brand leader, customers will associate the quality and reputation of their product with the leading brand.

b) Why are Kellogg's threatening legal action against Tesco?
Kellogg's believe that Tesco is imitating Kellogg's products. They may think that by doing this, Tesco is trying to benefit from Kellogg's reputation. Direct copying, without permission, of the Kellogg's brand name, graphics or logo is likely to be a breach of copyright. However, there have been cases where less direct imitation of a brand style has led to legal action.

Suggested answers unit 25

3. Which test used in *Times* corn flakes test?
Triangle test.

4. Why were bowls labelled A, B and C?
Suggestions might include:
- so that testers would not know there were only two different cereals being tested
- to keep the samples anonymous.

5. Why were tasters not allowed to add sugar to corn flakes?
Suggestions might include:
- addition of sugar alters flavour of cereal
- amount of sugar may vary meaning that test is not consistent.

6. Test a brand name product against own label versions.
Students could look back at the information in Unit 23 before carrying out this test.

Case Study
Design and packaging at Cadbury

Activities page 113

1. Why is company logo important?
It ensures instant recognition and reassures customers of quality.

2. Functions of confectionery pack.
Suggestions might include:
- aesthetic appeal
- protection against odour, moisture and flavour transfer
- contains the product to avoid loss
- displays the product attractively on shelf.

3. Examine packaging on a confectionery bar.
Students could look back at the information in Unit 25 before carrying out this activity.

4. a) How does confectionery packaging vary at Christmas and Easter?
Suggestions might include:
- may be more luxurious as products may be bought as gifts
- may have a seasonal decoration
- novelty packaging may be developed for the season only
- multi-packs may be available to encourage larger sales, e.g. stockings filled with different types of confectionery at Christmas.

b) Design seasonal confectionery package.
This activity allows students to use their imagination to design a seasonal confectionery package. If it is an appropriate time of year, you may wish to begin by comparing seasonal products available on the market. At other times of year, a class brainstorm will help students to remember products. Some students may feel more comfortable basing their design on an existing product, modifying it to make it suitable as a seasonal line. Students should consider manufacturing constraints and the importance of the corporate image.

unit 20 Planning work

Suggested answers

Activities page 115

Develop a new milk product to appeal to older children and teenagers.
The following suggestions may be helpful for this activity.
- A wide variety of resources should be made available to students to encourage experimentation.
- Discussion should help to eliminate any that may be too expensive or unrealistic!
- Savoury as well as sweet dishes should be considered.
- Milk shakes might be popular, but using yogurt or fromage frais could open up fresh possibilities.
- It is important that students work both as part of a team and as individuals. They must each have 'ownership' of part of the work and be able to dovetail their work in with the rest of the team.
- Dead lines should be clear and everyone must adhere to these. In a commercial environment, 'time is money'.
- The presentation of the idea is an integral part of the assignment, and all members of the team should participate.
- You may find the pro formas on pp. 114-21 useful.

unit 27

Working economically

Activities page 117

1. Does budget show that the business will make a profit or a loss?
A profit.

2. Sales needed to break even.
£373,600.

Activities page 118

1. Explain why it is a problem for bakery to hold:

a) too much stock.
Suggestions might include:
- capital tied up
- storage costs, e.g. refrigeration
- spoilage, e.g. stock kept beyond use by date.

b) not enough stock.
Suggestions might include:
- not having a vital ingredient for a recipe
- running out in the middle of a production run, thus wasting an entire batch.

2. Explain problem in following situations.

a) Bakery sells out of new bread.
Suggestions might include:
Problem
Not enough loaves have been produced by the bakery, either because demand was unexpected or because there were not enough ingredients to make more. The bakery should aim to fulfil demand without having a surplus. It is better to sell out than to have loaves left at the end of the day.

Possible solutions
- Stock take any left over goods at end of each day, re-ordering ingredients where necessary.
- Monitor sales carefully to find out how many loaves of cheese and tomato bread are needed.
- Increase output of cheese and tomato bread to fulfil increased demand.
- Adjust amounts of other breads made to balance the output.

b) Sandwich sales fall in cold weather.
Suggestions might include:
Problem
Sales of sandwiches are always much higher when the weather is warmer (because workers eat their lunch outside, people want a lighter snack, etc.) When the weather turns colder, sales of sandwiches fall because customers want hot, substantial lunches.

Possible solutions
- Offer toasted sandwiches in cold weather.
- Promote hot snacks instead, e.g. cheese and onion pasties, ham and egg flan.

c) Ingredients for fruit cake run out.
Suggestions might include:
Problem
The fruit cake is a product containing a large number of ingredients. There is always a chance that one of the ingredients may run out. This could be as a result of poor communication between baker and stock controller and more cakes being made than agreed.

Possible solutions
- Check stock carefully.
- Check standardised recipe is being used to ensure consistency. Correct if necessary.
- Devise an accurate purchasing specification for each recipe.
- Make sure that baker and stock controller agree about planned production and that baker informs stock controller of any change in plan in order to prevent waste.

Activities page 119

1. It costs the bakery 45p to produce each of their small loaves (regardless of type).

a) Why does bakery sell small white loaf for 40p?
The bakery is offering the loaf as a loss leader. It will make a loss on each loaf sold but hopes to encourage extra sales from customers who, having bought their cheap loaf, may buy other goods on impulse.

b) Why does bakery sell small granary loaf at 60p?
The granary loaf is considered more of a luxury item and customers may be willing to pay more. The greater profit made

51

unit 27 — Suggested answers

on the granary loaf helps the bakery to offset the loss made on the white loaf.

2. a) How many portions in gâteau?
12

b) How much should each slice sell for?

average cost of gâteau = £9.00
average cost of each slice = $\frac{900}{12}$ = 75p

selling price (depends on mark-up)
75p + e.g. 25p - 50p = £1.00 - £1.25

3. How much should bakery charge for a slice of pizza in order to compete with nearby takeaway?

average cost of pizza = £6.00
average cost of each slice = $\frac{600}{8}$ = 75p
competitor's selling price = 99p

The bakery's selling price could be from 76p to 98p. A figure of around 85p would probably be realistic.

Case Study
Film Cuisine

Activities page 120

1. Reasons for two catering units.
Allows company to work on more than one job at a time. Typically one unit is booked for film work (6-8 weeks work) while the other is free for smaller, more regular, jobs.

2. Advantages of buying meat ready portioned and frozen.
Suggestions might include:
- simpler to handle in a confined space
- defrosts more quickly
- cost effective, because chef uses only what is needed
- each piece hygienically sealed, not handled until just before cooking
- small pieces easier to store than larger.

3. Ten items from cash and carry.
Suggestions might include:
- cereals
- baked beans
- tinned tomatoes
- rice
- pasta
- fruit juices
- polystyrene cups
- napkins
- flour
- stock powder
- digestive biscuits
- individual packet cakes
- cream crackers
- jam
- pickle
- mayonnaise.

4. a) Tasks which need to be done by staff to prepare meals.
For breakfast, suggestions might include:
- put fruit juices in jugs
- set out the cereals, milk and sugar
- set out crockery and cutlery
- make porridge (in winter)
- grill bacon, sausages and vegetarian alternative
- prepare eggs (fried or scrambled)
- heat up tomatoes and beans
- make toast
- prepare tea and coffee
- serve breakfast
- clear away and wash up.

Students should approach other meals in a similar way.

b) Who would complete tasks?
Suggestions for breakfast might include:
- dining bus driver: sets out fruit juice, prepares coffee and tea, clears away
- chef: cooks eggs as and when required (sausages, bacon and vegetarian alternative cooked earlier and kept hot), serves
- assistant: prepares the rest of the breakfast, keeps toast replenished and helps to serve, washes up.

Students should approach other meals in a similar way.

5. Three hygiene rules staff should follow.
Suggestions might include:
- wash hands with warm water and anti-bacterial soap before touching food
- use separate chopping boards for raw and cooked foods
- cook food so that temperature at centre of food reaches a minimum of 70° for at least 2 minutes.

Any other reasonable suggestion concerning preparation, personal hygiene, or the care of the kitchen or dining area. Students could refer to Unit 9 - Food hygiene, Unit 19 - Using tools safely or Unit 30 - The law and the food industry.

6. Problems faced by film caterers.
Suggestions might include:
- space for preparation very limited
- number of diners could be large for such a small catering unit
- food must be prepared for everyone at the same time, rather than customers dropping in over a period of time

Suggested answers   unit 27

- meal may need to be made ready earlier than agreed or kept hot for longer
- electric power supply not always guaranteed, may need to use generators
- bottles of gas must be carried to fuel range
- water must be carried and disposed of hygienically
- waste must be stored and disposed of safely
- bad weather (e.g. problems with queuing customers, crowded dining bus, etc.)

Case Study
Automatic replenishment at United Biscuits

Activities page 121

1. How does ordering system at United Biscuits differ from other food manufacturers?

The Automatic Replenishment Package is a computer system which monitors levels of ingredients held in the United Biscuits' silos. The computer is linked by modem to the suppliers' terminals. Suppliers dial in at regular intervals to check the levels of the silos containing their products, giving them time to estimate how long before the silo will need topping up. This gives the supplier time to organise the next delivery. United Biscuits do not have to do any re-ordering.

2. What happens if ingredient reaches re-order levels?

If the level in the silo drops to re-order level, the Automatic Replenishment Package will automatically call the supplier.

3. How does ARP system reduce United Biscuits' costs?

Suggestions might include:

- saves time (no need for staff to carry out manual stock control)
- reduces administration costs (no need for staff to re-order stock)
- retains United Biscuits' capital for longer (stocks are only ordered - and paid for - as they are needed. This is called 'just-in-time' purchasing).

The first two reasons are likely to result in redundancies as staff are no longer needed to do certain jobs. You may wish to discuss this issue with students.

4. a) Advantages for suppliers.

Suggestions might include:

- suppliers have access to information about United Biscuits' needs - this allows them to plan their production and delivery schedules more efficiently
- suppliers know that they will get called in plenty of time for the next delivery
- suppliers are sure of a regular order from United Biscuits.

b) Disadvantages for suppliers.

Suggestions might include:

- suppliers have to install the computer system which could be costly
- the work previously done by United Biscuits (monitoring stock levels and re-ordering) is now the responsibility of the suppliers
- suppliers must be ready 24 hours to respond to the computer
- suppliers must have the ingredients ready for delivery when required.

unit 28 Systems

Suggested answers

Activities page 123

1. Draw systems diagram
Students can choose any type of diagram, e.g. mind map, flow chart, spider diagram. Figure 1 on p. 122 of students' book gives some ideas of the types of systems involved in the industrial manufacture of a product. Many of these areas are also relevant in domestic production (e.g. FINANCE: purchasing of materials; cost of energy used; overheads of running kitchen).

2. Inputs into lemon meringue pie system.
Suggestions might include:
- raw materials (e.g. flour, cornflour, fat, water, lemon juice/rind, egg yolk and white, sugar)
- information (e.g. market research on product, recipe, knowledge of prices of ingredients)
- energy (e.g. electric mixer to beat egg whites, manual stirring of lemon mixture, oven to bake pie).

3. Controls in the lemon meringue pie system.
Suggestions might include:
- test/check accuracy of scales to ensure accurate proportions
- switch to vary speed on electric mixer
- oven thermostat to control oven temperature.

Activities page 124

1. Production system used for wedding cakes.
Job production.

2. Advantages to customer of job production.
Suggestions might include:
- unique product
- high quality product
- can be tailor made to special requirements
- personal attention.

3. Costs involved in job production.
Students might discuss some of these points:
- special ingredients necessary, may only be used once
- labour intensive
- time consuming
- high cost per unit.

Activities page 125

1. a) Name production system used to make single sample of flavoured vinegar.
Job production.

b) What stages involved in making sample?
Suggestions might include:
- choose a flavour
- choose a suitable vinegar to be flavoured
- design a recipe for the sample
- make up a small quantity of the product
- marinate for required time before testing.

2. a) Suggest system for production of entire range.
Batch production.

b) Advantages of batch production.
Suggestions might include:
- suitable for production of small numbers of different products
- materials can be purchased in bulk
- costs lower than job production - spread over a number of products
- uses semi-skilled labour.

Disadvantages of batch production.
Suggestions might include:
- batch size must be accurate, or goods could remain unsold
- time lost between batches as machines reset
- costs higher than flow production
- risk of non-conformity between batches.

unit 29
Quality

Activities page 126

1. a) Questions to ask when judging quality of a product.
Students could use the brainstorm charts on pp. 131-2 to help them brainstorm ideas. Questions could be related to:
- taste
- appearance of product
- appearance of packaging
- smell
- ingredients used
- convenience
- value for money
- manufacturer's reputation
- environmental considerations, e.g. recyclability of packaging.

b) Check food product against quality control checklist.
Students could use the comparison pro forma on p. 112 to help them with this activity or they could add different headings.

2. Draw up quality control checklist for food products.
Checklists could include the following points:
- cheese and tomato sandwich - freshness and proportion of ingredients, even distribution of filling, safe preparation of foods
- ham and mushroom omelette - freshness and proportion of ingredients, safe preparation of foods, correct cooking time and temperature, immediate serving
- roast chicken, new potatoes, carrots and broccoli - freshness of ingredients, safe preparation of foods, vegetables similar size, correct cooking time and temperature, serving
- apple pie - freshness and proportion of ingredients, even thickness of pastry, even distribution of filling, correct cooking time and temperature, cooling and storage.

Activities page 127

1. List quality control checks used.
Visual inspection, metal detection, weight check.

2. What is purpose of these checks?
To identify any inferior peas, to detect foreign bodies and to ensure consistency of weight. These checks fulfil both quality control and legal requirements.

3. Draw a diagram of production process and indicate quality control measures.
Pupils could select either:
- a product they have made themselves
- a product they have seen produced in a commercial environment.

This activity could be supported with a video of commercial food production.

Case Study
Pizza production at McCain Foods

Activities page 128

1. Name some inputs into pizza production system.
Students could look back at Unit 28 to remind themselves of the input/process/output of a system.
Suggestions might include:
- raw materials, e.g. flour, yeast, water, cheese
- information, e.g. programming thermostats and time controls in equipment such as provers and ovens
- energy, e.g. power for ovens.

2. a) Points in production line where temperature is important.
Suggestions might include:
- frozen and chilled storage of ingredients
- dough making
- proving dough
- baking pizzas
- chilling pizzas
- freezing pizzas
- wrapping
- packing
- storing
- distribution.

b) How are computers used to help control temperature?

Computers are used to control temperature throughout the pizza production process (from dough mixing to base cooling). Thermostats within the equipment are linked to computers and are set to the correct temperature for each stage as set out in the specification. For more information on how thermostats work, students could look at the section on feedback in Unit 28, p. 123.

3. a) What manual checks are made?
Suggestions might include:
- microbiological analysis of ingredients on arrival
- pizza bases are inspected manually to check that they are the correct size, weight and that they are organoleptically acceptable
- sauce is tasted
- every hour, samples are cooked and tasted
- microbiological analysis of product before release from factory.

b) Why are manual checks important?
Suggestions might include:
- the human eye is an important judge of quality and consistency
- taste tests can only be carried out manually
- random sampling allows checks to be made on the performance of the product
- microbiological analysis ensures consumer safety.

4. What other products might be made by continual flow?

Products suitable for the continual flow system include anything which is added to as it goes through the production system.
Suggestions might include:
- gâteaux
- biscuits
- pies.

5. Simulate an assembly line.

Students might find the following pro formas helpful when planning this activity: brainstorm charts on pp. 131-2; planning schedule on p. 133.

Case Study
Heygates flour mill

Activities page 129

1. How does Heygates assure a quality product?
Suggestions might include:
- laboratory testing of wheat
- certificate of quality guarantee
- practical checks for consistency made in the experimental kitchen.

2. Suggest manufacturers who might buy flour from Heygates.
Suggestions might include:
- bread manufacturers
- local bakeries
- local restaurants.

3. Why does Heygates have an experimental kitchen?
Suggestions might include:
- allows regular testing of the flour produced in the mill
- assists customers who are experiencing difficulties with the product.

In addition, Heygates' experimental kitchen acts as an education resource for local schools and groups interested in bread production.

unit 30

The law and the food Industry

Activities page 130

1. Food Safety requirements mentioned in the article.

Food must not:
- injure the health of consumers
- be unfit
- be contaminated.

2. Invent two other cases involving offences under the Food Safety Act.

Any reasonable answer.

Activities page 132

1. Your opinion of the Café Vert's kitchen and storage areas.

Suggestions might include:
- not enough storage space, particularly fridge storage
- fridge is positioned next to meat preparation - risk of cross-contamination
- trade entrance, dumb waiter and stairs are dangerously positioned and could cause accidents
- sink and dishwasher - not enough workspace for cleaning and washing up
- inefficient planning of storage areas - resulting in excessive walking to obtain food from stores to preparation areas
- toilets should have double doors between them
- there should be lockers for staff outdoor clothing
- no sink for staff hand washing
- inappropriately situated range and grill - positioned in between preparation areas - thus breaking up the natural work flow.

2. Design a new layout

Any reasonable answer.

3. Three safety signs to displayed in the kitchen area.

For example:
- First aid
- Now wash your hands
- Fire exit.

Activities page 135

1. Questions an EHO might ask.

Suggestions might include:
- explain cleaning routines/rotas and deep cleaning procedures
- ask to see samples of food served and stored
- ask to see evidence of temperature monitoring, e.g. temperature probes and equipment
- ask to see pest control maintenance contracts
- ask to see equipment - in particular fridges, freezers, store rooms
- ask for evidence of stock control systems
- ask for evidence of staff training etc.

2. Four examples of good hygiene practice.

Suggestions might include:
- good hygiene training
- temperature monitoring equipment, e.g. probes
- good stock rotation
- evidence of good cleaning procedures including deep cleaning and clean premises.

3. What might happen if there is a food complaint to the EHO?

Likely process:
- EHO discuss the complaint with complainant
- EHO visit nursing home and take samples of food for testing
- EHO check premises to find out if food hygiene laws have been broken
- EHO keep complainant informed of progress of investigation
- EHO makes decision to proceed with formal or informal action.

57

unit 31 Risk assessment

Suggested answers

Activities page 136

1. How to explain risk assessment to fête organisers.

Students could mention some of the following:
- risk assessment a legal requirement
- must assess potential hazards involved in selling home made cakes
- must find out where hazards could occur
- must find out how hazards could be reduced.

In order to do this, the organisers should be aware of:
- the risks in storage and handling of foods they will sell
- which high risk products may be involved
- the effect of temperature, time and bacterial growth
- the need for food handlers to be instructed in personal hygiene and its importance in food sales.

2. Draw a flow chart of the stages in production and sale of cakes.

Suggested stages:
- buy ingredients for cakes at wholesalers
- transport ingredients
- store appropriately, i.e. cupboards/fridges
- make cakes
- wrap cakes
- sell to customer.

3. Identify critical control points in process.

Students could present their ideas in the form of a table, for example:
See Table 10.

Activities page 137

Hazards in production of roast chickens

Table 11 shows some possible suggestions.

Activities page 139

These activities could be based on a recent practical session, or on the industrial manufacture of a food product that students have seen on a visit or video.

You could divide students into groups with responsibility for the following: raw food, cooking process and serving/storage.

For brainstorming activities such as discussing potential hazards and identifying appropriate controls, students could use the brainstorm charts on pp. 131-2.

Table 10

CRITICAL CONTROL POINTS	CONTROLS
Buy ingredients	1. Buy quality products from reputable stores. 2. Check ingredients stored at correct temperature in store. 3. Check use by dates.
Transport ingredients	1. Ensure rapid transfer of high risk foods. 2. Could use cool bags/boxes.
Store ingredients	Store at correct temperature.
Make cakes	1. Ensure awareness of personal and food hygiene. 2. Cook at correct temperatures and for correct time.
Wrap cakes	1. Use hygienic materials. 2. Seal correctly. 3. List ingredients and use by date.
Sell cakes	Ensure serving staff aware of personal and food hygiene.

Table 11

1. HAZARD	2. WHERE	3. CONTROLS
Inadequate defrosting	Defrosting	Allow enough time for thorough defrosting in a fridge.
Inadequate cooking	Cooking	1. Check and control oven temperature. 2. Ensure adequate cooking time.
Storage temperature after cooking not high enough	Hot holding	Check and control temperature in hot tray.

Suggested answers

unit 31

Case Study: Designing hygienic kitchens

Activities page 140

Suitable wall covering for 'The Lite Bite'.

Wall behind food preparation area:
- food preparation areas must be easily cleaned and non porous
- low to medium budget suggest tiles, PVC/GRP sheeting
- higher budget suggest stainless steel sheeting.

Wall behind oven, grill and hob:
- again must be easily cleaned and non porous
- should be resistant to high temperatures
- suggest tiles or stainless steel sheeting (not too expensive for this small area).

Wall in customer services area:
- aesthetic appeal important
- could use coloured tiles or acrylic polymer.

Higher parts of wall:
- walls above 1.80m do not need to be so durable
- could continue tiles or use cheaper acrylic polymer.

Case Study: HACCP in Burnaby Hospital

Activities page 141

1. Importance of identifying hazards before food consumption.

Reduce risk of contamination, which could be critical in a hospital, as sick people more vulnerable to infection from food poisoning bacteria.

2. Information to be included in a recipe to help prevent food safety hazards.

Suggestions might include:
- specify equipment to be used (e.g. separate chopping boards to avoid cross contamination)
- specify temperature and time for cooking
- specify temperature that centre of products must reach (use temperature probes)
- specify maximum cooling time
- specify storage temperatures and maximum storage times.

3. How does hospital check cleaning and sanitation procedures are followed?

Suggestions might include:
- written procedures for cleaning and equipment sanitation
- random microbiological checks on equipment, workers, work surfaces and utensils.

4. How does hospital monitor time/temperature relationship in cook-chill process?

Suggestions might include:
- specifies minimum time/temperature for centre of cooked food (checked with thermometer or probe)
- specifies cooling temperature and time
- controls storage temperature with alarms.

5. Importance of staff understanding HACCP system.

Suggestions might include:
- staff understand principle of providing safe food for others
- all staff contribute to overall safety.
- every member of staff has responsibility for setting and maintaining standards
- only one mistake could cause a food safety hazard.

Section 2

Planned activities

Planned activities for Design and Technology - Food

Introduction
This section includes suggested lessons designed to:
- reinforce and develop skills learned in Key Stage 3 and to provide a basis for further study in food and technology related subjects
- encourage independent learning within the technology structure by developing confidence skills and ability at all levels
- offer ideas and opportunities for interactive learning
- assist with documentation which will satisfy the National Curriculum orders.

Organisation of lessons
Lessons have been provided in two styles.

1. A lesson by lesson scheme, giving aims, learning outcomes, suggestions for content, resources required and homework tasks. This scheme could be a framework on which to base more detailed lesson plans if required. The complete scheme could account for one term's work and includes differentiated questions on which to base assessment decisions. The scheme covers the technology process as follows:

Lesson 1	Design brief and task analysis
Lessons 2 and 3	Research
Lessons 4 and 5	Generation of possible solution
Lesson 6	Specification and development of solutions.
Lesson 7	Application of industrial processes
Lesson 8	Planning and production of outcome
Lesson 9	Evaluation
Lesson 10	Assessment.

2. A series of six lesson matrices. This more flexible approach enables both staff and pupils to develop the briefs provided to suit their own needs, resources and capabilities. By using each matrix at some point during Key Stage 4 teachers will ensure coverage of skills, knowledge and understanding as specified in the Design and Technology programmes of study. A set of differentiated questions has been provided to support the teaching and learning in each area.

Mapping and monitoring
It is important to monitor lesson content against the programmes of study in order to analyse the frequency of skills used. There will inevitably be repetition especially with planning and making skills. The mapping pro forma on p. 140 will enable staff to record programmes of study delivered within the units. This will help to avoid unnecessary repetition, and to facilitate a comprehensive coverage of the syllabus.

Assessment
Teachers need to decide which aspects of the lesson or unit are to be assessed prior to delivery.

Using the students' textbook
Case studies and unit content will complement, enhance and support the work in the teachers' guide.

Key experiences and skills
Lessons have been produced as a progressive series which enables students to:
- increase knowledge, skills and understanding
- move from familiar to unfamiliar concepts
- gradually develop more complex solutions
- focus on the composition and function of a range of food products.

Lessons cover the whole technology process including:
- planning, organising and managing skills
- designing skills
- making skills
- food product design, manufacturing and processing
- the analysis of food as a material.

Teacher information
Italics indicate extra information for teachers and need not necessarily be reproduced if lesson plans are required by the management team of the school.

Differentiation
Work is differentiated by:
- outcome - same task, varying response
- task - different task and different levels of difficulty in the same task
- resource - use of different resources in terms of variety and/or level
- classroom organisation - independent, paired or group work.

Information technology
Lessons allow scope for development and application of I.T. skills in the following areas:
- assisted learning
- CAD/CAM
- data display
- investigations
- monitoring and control
- research
- simulations.

Cross-curricular links
In addition to I.T. applications, lessons provide the opportunity to develop competence in communications and numeracy. Links are also possible with art and design, business studies and science.

Planned activities — Introduction

VOCABULARY

Term or phrase	Alternative/explanation
Materials and components	Ingredients, food commodities
Material functions	Choice of ingredients, food characteristics, suitability for purpose
Processing	Preparation for manufacture
Primary processing	First stage processing, e.g. milling
Secondary processing	Second stage processing, e.g. bread
Systems	Methods of domestic or commercial production
Control	Factors which monitor the production process, e.g. oven thermostats
Input	Information required to start a system
Process	How the system works
Output	Product made by a system
Design brief	Instruction to develop an idea from an initial concept - involving research, analysis, specification, generation of ideas, development of solution, planning and production of outcome, evaluation
Making skills	To create a finished product using appropriate equipment and skills
Performance criteria	Identified assessment objectives
Food as a material	Working with a range of foods in order to gain knowledge and understanding based on food properties and characteristics
Range	Aspects of knowledge, e.g. key design features, aesthetic and performance characteristics, production constraints
Task analysis	Identifying needs and opportunities
Specification	A detailed written plan of design requirements
Generation of ideas	Individual or group brainstorm leading to a consensus of opinion
Development of solution	Modification of ideas
Production of outcome	Practical activity leading to the creation of a product
Evidence indicators	Work produced by a pupil which acts as proof of knowledge and understanding, e.g. written work, presentations, answers to verbal questioning
Core skills	Skills which should be integrated into design work and assessed. Numeracy, written, verbal and visual communication, I.T.
Material	Ingredients, food commodities

Lesson scheme

All about sauces

An initial project which is simple, directed and with little student planning.

Aims
To establish examination procedures and logical work patterns.

Objectives
Students to understand how to work through a project covering all the criteria as laid down in the examination syllabi.

Design brief
Design a new sauce which could be commercially produced and create a dish with which it could be used.

Sauces — **Planned activities**

Lesson 1 — Design brief and task analysis

Design brief
Design a new sauce which could be commercially produced and create a dish with which it could be used.

Aims
To introduce the topic to the class and to establish a pattern for the analysis of research.

Outcomes
Students to understand:
- the brief
- the D & T terminology 'task analysis' (see Vocabulary on p. 61)
- how to begin tackling a brief through discussion in a group.

Resources
Pro formas on pp. 131-2 and p. 110.
Some samples of sauces as a trigger start.

Introduction
What the lesson is going to cover and what the students can expect to contribute.

Issue brief.
Brainstorm.
Design a survey.
Draw conclusions from results.

Teaching and learning strategies
Main part of the lesson should include positive discussion between students and teacher.

Brainstorm
Use either brainstorm chart on p. 131 or p. 132.
Suggestions for discussion:
- What is a sauce? How does it differ from a dressing?
- Establish various target groups - sociological and cultural.
- Compare cost of existing products.
- Compare quantity provided by existing products (number of portions per unit).
- How to establish the most popular flavours? (Survey, using questionnaire pro forma on p. 110.)

Planned activities   **Sauces**

Teaching and learning strategies (continued)

Survey

Suggestions:
- Do you use ready prepared sauces?
- What with (e.g. chicken, mince, Quorn)?
- What types do you use?
- Which are your family's favourites?
- Are jars, cans or chilled sauces the most frequently purchased?
- Which brands have been tried within the group

Questions to be planned by students.

Conclusion

Re-cap on the terminology. Summarise how the work has progressed and what has to be completed before the next lesson, or time to be agreed. Students should be aware of the importance of completing the work to the highest standard.

Homework

Questionnaire pro formas to be prepared and completed. Suggest that ten people should be questioned, e.g. teachers, neighbours, relatives, students. Students should draw conclusions from their results and be ready to share their ideas in the following lesson.

Staff comments

It is suggested that after each lesson some notes should be made on the good and the bad points of the lesson so that you can adjust for another year.

Sauces | **Planned activities**

Lesson 2 — Research

Aims
To analyse some ready made sauces through disassembly.

Outcomes
Students to:
- work as part of a group to disassemble the sauce provided
- be able to report their findings back to the group
- write up their results in appropriate form.

Resources
Paper/exercise books.
Samples of bottled, chilled or dried sauces which have obvious component parts, e.g. peppers, onions, carrots, etc.
Equipment for disassembly.
Food Technology Unit 24.
Product specification pro forma on p. 114 for recording disassembly findings.

Introduction
What the lesson will achieve and how the students will be expected to work.

Disassembly
Working as a team each group will:
- disassemble one product
- find the nutritional information on the packet, copy and compare the information with other groups, be ready to report back to own group and class
- use ingredients list on packet to help those disassembling the sauce, draw conclusions and write them up
- record cost and draw conclusions about: quantity and quality.

Teaching and learning strategies
Main part of the lesson should be student centred with teacher helping to keep the focus when necessary. Some disassembly may need teacher guidance.

Students should be able to work as groups to produce an evaluation of their sauce using the criteria set out in the introduction of the lesson. Students must be aware that the reporting back process is important so that everyone can share their experiences.

Planned activities — Sauces

Conclusion
Teacher to re-cap the main points raised in the feedback period.

Give a verbal evaluation of each group's work. Comment on the standard of feedback and the method chosen.

Homework
Complete the write up in an appropriate way, i.e. by hand or using a word processor. Photographs could be used.

Staff comments

Sauces   **Planned activities**

Lesson 3 — Research

Aims
To conduct a blind tasting.
To establish objective results to the tasting.

Outcomes
Students to understand the need for objective tasting when preparing a new product for the market.

Resources
A range of commercially bought tomato sauces.
Blindfolds.
Spoons and bowls for tasting.
Glasses/water for palate cleansing.
Food Technology Unit 23.

Introduction
An explanation of how the tasting of the sauces is to be achieved, depending on school resources. Tasting in isolation and blindfolded would be ideal. Adapt to suit.
- Introduce sauces to the group.
- Reinforce ground rules for tasting.

Teaching and learning strategies
Ensure each student is properly equipped, and understands the disciplines for tasting panels. If tasting lessons have not been covered at Key Stage 3, it would be advisable to carry out taste testing training sessions.

Students should carry out the tasting following the rules laid down. Results to be recorded with care - should include:
- texture
- aroma
- flavour.

Conclusion
The results of the tasting should be available at this stage of the lesson.

Responses should be discussed as a group. Comparisons should be made with the results of the initial survey and conclusions drawn.

Homework
Complete the report on the lesson's work.

Staff comments

Planned activities — **Sauces**

Lesson 4

Generation of possible solution

Aims
To introduce the students to sauce making, through a demonstration.
To encourage student development of a basic recipe design.
Students to present proposed design as a flow chart in readiness for a trial run.

Outcomes
Students to:
- know and understand how a sauce can be made
- pinpoint critical control points during teacher demonstration
- brainstorm alternative flavours and to design own sauce recipe.

Resources
Shopping order, recipe, brainstorm charts and flow chart on p. 122, p. 123, pp. 131-2 and p. 134
Materials for demonstration of sauce.
Recipe books or cards to trigger students.
Food Technology p. 67.
Optional - I.T. facilities.

Development and generation of ideas

Introduction
The demonstration may cover any of the basic sauces, but should give scope for additions or variations. Could continue the theme of tomato sauces.

Teacher to explain how the lesson will develop, and to emphasise the importance of following the demonstration with care, so that critical control points can be established.

Teaching and learning strategies

- Demonstration (students to use recipe pro forma).
- Emphasise critical control points (weighing and measuring, storage, temperature control - cooking, hygiene - personal and equipment, quality control).
- Brainstorm alternative flavours.
- Discuss ideas.
- Design own sauce recipe.
- Present as a flow chart
- Consider viability of commercial production.

Teacher needs to give strategies for problem solving, e.g. avoiding a lumpy sauce; removing tomato skins; avoiding burning; maintaining a standard consistency; avoiding a raw taste.

Sauces — Planned activities

Conclusion
Consolidate the work completed by the students together. Ensure they understand they are trialling their own sauce in the next lesson.

Homework
Preparing for the practical.

Staff comments

Planned activities | **Sauces**

Lesson 5

Generation of possible solution

Aims
Students to trial their own design and evaluate.
Students to self evaluate their own hygiene and safety procedures.

Outcomes
Students to:
- discover through experience if their design is practicable
- complete their own self evaluation chart on hygiene and safety.

Resources
Hygiene and safety pro forma on p. 118.
Spare ingredients for emergencies.
Optional - I.T. facilities.

Introduction
Re-cap the aim of the practical is to discover if the sauce designed will be acceptable. Suggest to students that they should begin to think of the criteria they could use to establish this.

Teaching and learning strategies
- Students to prepare their sauces.
- Students should consider if the sauce could be reheated:
    in a microwave
    on the hob
    in the oven.

Conclusion
Students to:
- write an evaluation of the practical
- state any changes required to design
- state if, in their opinion, the sauce would be commercially viable.

Homework
Complete the write up and decide if there needs to be another attempt at making an adapted sauce. Let the member of staff know in plenty of time!

Staff comments

Sauces Planned activities

Lesson 6

Specification and development of solution

Aims
Students to finalise their recipe designs, and write up the specification.
Students to prepare information for the product label.

Outcomes
Students to:
- revise the original recipe design, through practical work if necessary
- prepare product labels, to include: nutritional content; ingredients list; serving suggestions; cost; suitability for vegetarians; number of servings; and best before date.

Resources
Food Technology Unit 25.
Visual design planner pro formas on pp. 125-6.
Optional - I.T. facilities.

Introduction
Summarise the work done so far. Remind the group of the original objective, i.e. to produce a new sauce for the market, which could be successfully produced commercially. This lesson is to finalise their **design solution** to the brief and produce a **specification** for the product. Remind students of the regulations regarding labelling and the need to ensure their product displays this information. Students to research and design the label during this lesson.

Teaching and learning strategies
- Practical to commence if needed.
- Final design specification to be recorded.
- Students to prepare product labels to include:
    - nutritional content
    - ingredients list
    - serving suggestions
    - cost
    - suitability for vegetarians
    - number of servings
    - best before date.

Planned activities

Sauces

Conclusion
The students should be collecting together a good portfolio of work. Ensure all is in chronological order, properly headed and illustrated.

Homework
Complete all work to date either by hand or word processor.

Staff comments

Sauces

Lesson 7 — Industrial practices

Planned activities

Aims
To translate designs into mass production specifications.
To consider problems which might arise with the specifications.

Outcomes
Using a flow chart, students translate their domestic product into an industrial context.

Resources
Flow chart pro forma on p. 134.
Food Technology Units 26, 28, 29, 31.
Optional I.T. facilities.

Introduction
Introduce industrial practices. Use students' book to cover this section.

Teaching and learning strategies
Students to produce flow chart to show:
- goods into factory
- process
- packaging
- storage
- transportation
- critical control points.

Students to identify three problems which may be experienced by a food manufacturer of ready made sauces and offer solutions.

Consider:
- *guaranteed supply of imported components*
- *transportation costs*
- *the range of sauces possible*
- *machinery required, e.g. for skinning tomatoes*
- *choice of tomato variety, flavour, colour, and size*
- *need to guarantee hygienic delivery of raw materials*
- *maintenance of temperature control (computer monitored)*
- *staff training.*

Planned activities **Sauces**

Conclusion
Identify any problems which are similar in domestic and industrial contexts.

Homework
Look for good sources of tomatoes:
- in the supermarket
- in geography text books
- using computer encyclopaedia.

Copy out original flow chart neatly for portfolio.
Plan and prepare for final practical - using sauce design to complete serving suggestion from Lesson 6.

Staff comments

Sauces — **Planned activities**

Lesson 8 — Planning and production

Aims
To finalise sauce making action plan.
To design a completed dish using the sauce.

Outcomes
Students to prepare their dish from the homework plan.

Resources
Camera to record final product.

Planning and production of outcome
Students to ensure they have completed product specifications in line with design brief, prior to making.

Conclusion
Students, as a group, to evaluate each other's work.

Homework
Evaluation and conclusion after the dish has been consumed.

Staff comments

Planned activities   **Sauces**

Lesson 9

Evaluation

Aims
To conclude series of lessons on sauces with an evaluation of skills, processes, planning and production.

Outcomes
Students to identify factors which caused them to modify ideas or change their plans. The evaluation should make reference to the brief and should include recommendations for improvement in terms of planning, materials and process.

Resources
All work completed to date including charts, graphs, pro formas and photographs.
Planning schedule pro forma on p. 133.
Complete evaluation sheets on pp. 119-20.
Optional I.T. facilities.

Introduction
Re-cap on stages of the design brief, encouraging students to consider their own performance at each stage.

Teaching and learning strategies
Use the pro formas to highlight and reinforce the examination terminology and the sequence of work essential for the technology process.

Conclusion
All work to be completed before assessment can take place.

Homework
Revision for test.

Staff comments

Sauces — **Planned activities**

Lesson 10

Assessment

Aims
To assess technological development and recall via:
- the formulation and presentation of a completed design portfolio
- production of an appropriate, quality outcome
- formal testing procedures.

Students will experience examination style questions related to the current lesson scheme.

Outcomes
Students will test the level of their acquired skills and knowledge.

Staff comments

Planned activities **Sauces**

Lesson Scheme 1 Questions

Section A

Total - 30 marks

The questions have been divided into three differentiated sections, which may be used separately or consecutively, depending on the student's ability.

1. You are planning to use a ready prepared sauce with chicken.
   Name five sauces which you could use. **(2½ marks)**

2. The diagrams below show the packaging for three different types of sauce.

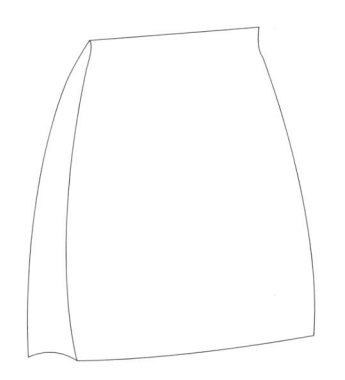

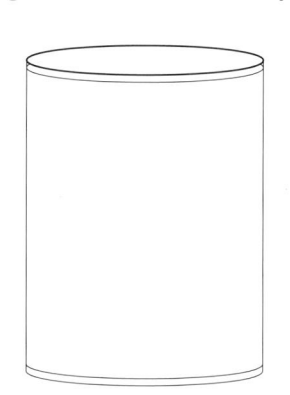

   Name a sauce which is likely to be sold in each of the packages. **(3 marks)**

3. Using the diagrams below design the packaging for the front and the back of the jar. **(5 marks)**

4. What other foods would you add to the chicken dish to complete the meal?
   Give a reason for each. **(2 marks)**

5. Name an alternative to chicken in your dish and give one reason for your choice. **(2 marks)**

Sauces **Planned activities**

6. What factors may influence a consumer when selecting ready prepared sauces? **(3 marks)**

7. Give two reasons why the market in ready made sauces is expanding. **(2 marks)**

8. Why might a company decide to launch a new sauce product? **(2 marks)**

9. How will the company decide on the components to be used, the recipe and the cost? **(2 marks)**

10. Here is a list of familiar dishes. Which ones could be made using ready made sauces? **(3 marks)**
- spaghetti bolognese
- chicken casserole
- fish pie
- beef stew
- vegetable curry
- quiche lorraine
- lamb samosa
- macaroni cheese
- sausage pie.

11. Explain, with examples, how the needs of different cultures have been considered in the ready made sauce market.

(3 ½ marks)

Section B

Total - 25 marks

12. Here are some comments made by a taste panel testing sauces:
- too bland
- too salty
- too thick
- too brightly coloured
- too runny.

How could adaptions be made to overcome these criticisms? **(10 marks)**

13. List four food materials in a sauce you have studied and state their functions in the product.

(8 marks)

14. In the production of a tomato based sauce, why is it desirable/necessary to remove the skins?

(2 marks)

15. Look at these two labels for a tomato based sauce.

Planned activities **Sauces**

SAUCE A	SAUCE B
tomatoes, water, onions, modified starch, sugar, chillies, lemon juice, salt	water, tomato purée, tomatoes, peppers, onions, salt, sugar, oil

a) Which sauce would have the more intense tomato flavour? (1 mark)
b) Which one has more salt? (1 mark)
c) Which one would be thicker? (1 mark)
d) Which one would be more red in colour? (1 mark)
e) Which one would contain more NSP? (1 mark)

Section C

Total - 50 marks

16. Look at the flow chart for a traditionally made roux based sauce.

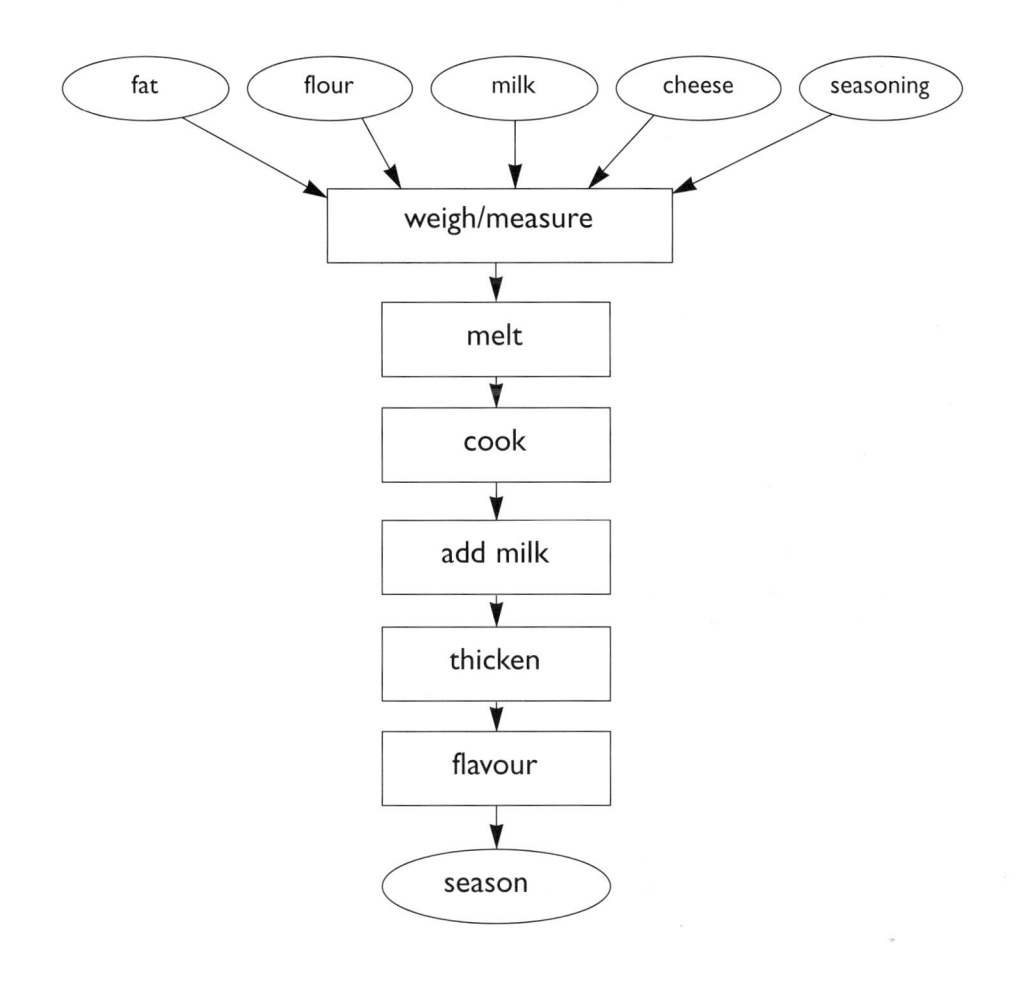

fat, flour, milk, cheese, seasoning → weigh/measure → melt → cook → add milk → thicken → flavour → season

Sauces   Planned activities

a) Name two types of fat which could be used to make the sauce. **(1 mark)**
b) Suggest alternative components which would lower the fat content of the sauce. **(1 mark)**
c) Why is the cooking process necessary? **(2 marks)**
d) Explain the importance of adding the milk gradually. **(2 marks)**
e) This traditional process can be modified to save time. Draw a flow chart to show the all in one method of making a white sauce. How will this method save time?
(5 marks)
f) Which process would be more appropriate for mass production? Give reasons for your choice.
(2 marks)
g) State two stages at which hygiene checks should take place. **(2 marks)**
h) State two stages at which quality control checks should take place. **(2 marks)**

17. The consistency of a sauce is important. Explain the effect on the consumer of:
a) a sauce that has a high proportion of water in it **(4)**
b) a thick sauce. **(4)**
Consider flavour, value for money and cooking performance in your answer. **(8 marks)**

18. A sauce manufacturer is considering the following marketing strategies:
a) using the sauce in a cookery series hosted by a famous televison chef **(2)**
b) using prime time television for a humorous advertisement **(2)**
c) using 'two for the price of one' purchase offers **(2)**
d) offering a free recipe book with four product labels. **(2)**
Evaluate in detail the strengths and weaknesses of each idea. **(8 marks)**

19. A small café is considering putting sausage casserole on the menu.
a) What points need to be considered when deciding if a ready prepared sauce should be used? **(3)**
b) Do you consider it a wise production decision to use a ready prepared sauce in the casserole? Explain your answer. **(2)**
c) What effect will the variety and quality of the sausage have on the end product? **(3)**
d) How could the café vary the sausage casserole to make it suitable for vegetarians? **(2)**
e) Devise a system for producing the casserole. Note the critical control points. **(4)**
f) How could the café judge the success of its new menu addition? **(3)**

(17 marks)

Planned activities

Sauces

Lesson scheme Answers

Section A

1. Any appropriate answer including any of the curry flavours or any tomato based sauce. Suggestions might include:
   - 'Chicken Tonight'
   - Tikka Masala
   - Korma
   - Spanish
   - Sweet and Sour
   - Barbecue.

2. Suggestions might include:
   - pouch - pesto, cheese
   - can - curries, red and white wine sauces, barbecue
   - jar - cream based sauces, tomato based sauces.

3. The following could be included:
   - name of product
   - ingredients
   - storage instructions
   - instructions for use
   - use by or best before date
   - lot or batch code
   - bar code
   - serving suggestion
   - name and address of manufacturer
   - country of origin.

4. Additional foods should include sources of carbohydrate and vegetables, which provide a variety of textures and colours.

5. Alternatives to chicken could be any other appropriate meat or fish. Students may also consider a variety of vegetables.

6. Factors which may influence a consumer include:
   - price
   - value for money
   - flavour
   - versatility of the sauce
   - nutritional value
   - how the product has been marketed.

7. Reasons for an expanding sauce market could be:
   - demand for home cooked meals, which are quick and easy to prepare
   - requirement for authentic flavours without the inconvenience of buying individual components.

8. A company may decide to launch a new sauce:
   - to improve its market position
   - as a response to consumer demand
   - as part of a launch of several new sauces.

9. The choice of components, recipe and cost will be decided through market research and product testing at each stage of the development process. See Unit 22 in the students' book.

10. Ready made sauces could be used in the following dishes:
    - spaghetti bolognese
    - chicken casserole
    - fish pie
    - beef stew
    - vegetable curry
    - macaroni cheese.

11. Other cultures have been considered in the ready made sauce market by introducing ranges such as:
    - Indian
    - Thai
    - Mexican
    - Chinese.

Section B

12. Adaptions might include:
    - **Too bland** - more flavouring required, this could be basic seasoning or the introduction of components with a more pronounced flavour such as garlic, chilli, coriander etc. The recipe may need modification, e.g. frying onions before adding them to the dish in order to add the typical caramel flavour.
    - **Too salty** - salt content needs to be reduced, components may need adjustment, e.g. using a milder cheese or a non-smoked bacon. Monosodium glutamate may need to be reduced or omitted.
    - **Too thick** - the consistency of the product needs modification by reducing the proportion of thickening agents and/or increasing the liquid in the product.
    - **Too runny** - the consistency of the product needs modification by reducing the proportion of liquid and/or adding more thickening possibly in the form of modified starch.
    - **Too brightly coloured** - the amount of artificial colouring needs to be reduced. This comment is unlikely if colourings come from natural sources.

13. Suggestions for components and their functions in the product might include:

Sauces — Planned activities

- tomatoes - main ingredient
- oil - extra flavour
- modified starch - thickener
- water - used together with thickener to extend product (see answer to Q17a).

14. Tomato skins should be removed because:
- they could be a source of infection
- they create an unappealing texture within the product.

15. a) Sauce B would have the more intense flavour.

b) Sauce B has more salt.

c) Sauce A may be thicker as it has the addition of an artificial thickener in the form of modified starch. It also has a higher proportion of tomatoes which may act as a natural thickener.

d) Sauce B may be redder in colour due to the addition of tomato purée as well as tomatoes. The purée has a more concentrated colour.

e) Sauce B may have more NSP as it contains a variety of vegetables.

Section C

16. a) Alternative fats are:
- butter
- margarine.

b) Components which would lower the fat content are:
- low fat spread
- low fat cheese
- skimmed milk.

c) The cooking process is necessary in order to cook the starch grains which have absorbed the milk and thickened the sauce. Adequate cooking is essential to avoid a raw flavour.

d) Adding the milk gradually allows gradual absorption by the starch grains and avoids lumps.

e) The traditional process can be modified by using the all in one method.

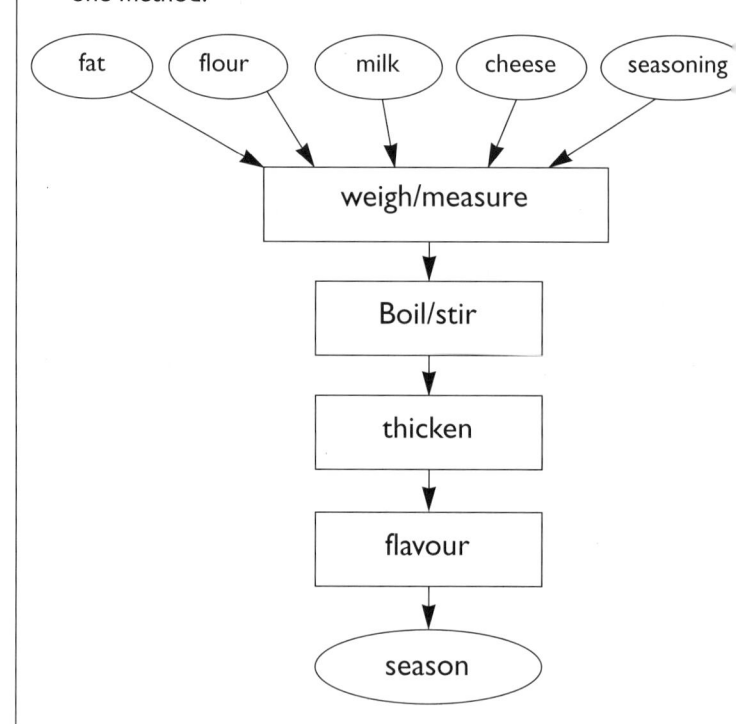

```
fat   flour   milk   cheese   seasoning
   ↘    ↘     ↓     ↙       ↙
         weigh/measure
              ↓
           Boil/stir
              ↓
            thicken
              ↓
            flavour
              ↓
            season
```

f) The all in one method would be better for mass production as it saves time and labour.

g) Hygiene checks should take place:
- at the beginning of the process - to ensure that the food preparation environment and the handler do not contaminate the food
- throughout production - equipment and processes should be monitored to avoid infection
- after production - hygiene checks should involve the appropriate storage of the product to avoid cross-contamination.

h) Suggestions for quality control checks might include:
- visual inspection of components to ensure freshness and quality
- tasting finished sauce to ensure it conforms to the specification in terms of flavour and consistency
- passing finished product through a metal detector to ensure no foreign objects.

17. a) Effect on consumer of sauce with a high proportion of water:
- may have a less intense flavour
- may have a thin consistency and could lack flavour
- if it is a ready made product it may be regarded as being of poorer quality
- dishes made with a 'thin' sauce may require thickening after the cooking process.

Planned activities

Sauces

b) Effect on consumer of thicker sauce:
- may be considered a better quality product
- may appear to be creamy in texture
- care should be taken when cooking as thicker sauces can dry out if the cooking time is exceeded
- foods requiring a moist cooking environment e.g. no pre-cook required pasta may be tough and unpalatable
- additional liquid may be added to thicker sauces to extend the product.

18. a) Using the sauce in a cookery series:
- television exposure for product
- brand name may not be mentioned on the programme
- audience tightly targeted, i.e. those interested in cooking
- audience could be limited, i.e. people at home when the programme is aired.

b) Advertisement on prime time television:
- ensures maximum exposure for the product, its brand name and performance
- humour ensures the product is recalled when the consumer is shopping
- expensive option.

c) Two for the price of one offers:
- effective marketing tool if the product is already established on the market
- useful follow-up to a television campaign
- boosts sales.

d) Recipe book marketing strategy:
- informs the manufacturer about consumer loyalty
- may be an additional incentive to buy for established consumers
- may not attract new consumers
- relatively inexpensive option for manufacturer.

19. a) Evaluation of using a ready prepared sauce.

STRENGTHS	WEAKNESSES
Ensures consistent product	Does not allow for chef's creativity
Saves time in preparation/cooking	Can be more expensive
Little or no cooking skill required	Must ensure the product is continually available

b) Students should give their own view, based on personal experience of using ready prepared sauces. Any appropriate and justified answer is acceptable.

c) The variety and quality of the sausage used is important in determining the appeal of the finished product.
- The café may choose a sausage with a coarse texture or one with added herbs or spices. This will add character to the dish and will affect the cost of each portion.
- A sausage with a high proportion of fat will alter the flavour and nutritional value of the dish.
- Decisions need to be made about whether to have skinned or skinless sausages. The texture of the skin needs to be compatible with the dish.
- Cheaper sausages with a high proportion of filler, preservatives and additives will affect flavour and texture.
- The café may consider blends of meat in the sausage or speciality sausages e.g. venison.

d) The casserole could be made suitable for vegetarians by:
- using vegetarian sausages
- adding a variety of vegetables and beans to the sauce.

e) Suggestion for system for producing the casserole.

ACTION	CRITICAL CONTROL POINTS
Assemble components and equipment required	Appropriate storage prior to use
Wash hands	Hygiene
Fry/grill sausages until brown	
Place sausages in casserole dish	
Pour over sauce	
Bake	Correct time and temperature
Cool	Correct cooling time before refrigeration/freezing
Store	Correct storage temperature
Serve	

f) The success of the sausage casserole could be judged by:
- number of people choosing dish
- repeat orders on subsequent visits
- amount of waste
- asking the consumers if they enjoyed the meal
- asking consumers to complete a short questionnaire
- asking them to rate dish on a scale of 1-10.

Fruit and vegetables — Planned activities

Fruit and vegetables — Teaching matrix 1

	Students' book reference	Learning outcomes	Suggested activities
Food focus Fruit and vegetables	Unit 3 Unit 17 page 65	Awareness of the range of fruit and vegetables available. Awareness of cooking methods.	1. Analyse ready made salads available in shops and supermarkets. 2. Compare the range of stir fry packs available. Focus on value for money and convenience. 3. Investigate the range of potato products available which have special appeal for small children. 4. Compare the variety of ready prepared chips available. 5. Working as a taste panel, carry out a tasting using Wacky Vegetables from Iceland. Assess their performance and popularity. 6. Using food tables, calculate the vitamin C content of a fruit salad containing both kiwi fruit and oranges. 7. Using food tables or a computer programme, create a graph which shows the relative NSP content of a range of fruit and vegetables both raw and cooked. 8. Carry out a sensory analysis of a range of carrots, e.g. organic, value brand, etc. **Ideas for practicals** *30 minute meals which might include:* • stir fry dish • vegetable kebab • crudités and dips • unusual salads • vegetable pasta dishes
Nutrient focus Vitamins Minerals NSP Fats	pages 14-15 Unit 6 pages 24, 55-6 Unit 4	Understanding of the value of fruit and vegetables in the diet. Knowledge of the vitamin and mineral content of specific fruit and vegetables. Knowledge of NSP and its importance in the diet. Understanding of the composition of fats	
Skills, knowledge and understanding Food hygiene Cooking methods Product development Combining and shaping Loss of vitamin C Preparation and cleaning Enzymic browning Safety Emulsions	Unit 9 page 16, Table 6 page 102 page 65 pages 14-15, 16, 28 page 16, Table 5 page 16 Unit 19 pages 18-19	A continuing development of manipulative skills, e.g. using knives. Increasing knowledge and skills when using electrical equipment. Development of combining and shaping skills, e.g. sauces, chutneys and potato chips. Development of analysis and evaluation in comparison activities. Development of research techniques. Development of an understanding of emulsifying agents used in food.	

Planned activities — Fruit and vegetables

Design briefs	Assessment	Opportunities	Cross-curricular
1. Design a 'salad in a tub' with a mayonnaise or vinaigrette dressing. 2. Design a dish which will encourage small children to eat vegetables. 3. Design a fruit based lunch box snack for a 'fruitarian'. 4. Design a simple dessert for an elderly person, using fruits in season. 5. Design a preserve suitable for marketing in National Trust outlets. 6. Design suitable menus for a week with adequate quantities of NSP and vitamin C for a pregnant woman.	Teacher assessment of: 1. Response to written questions and written activities. 2. Response to verbal questioning. 3. Observation and assessment of working methods and skill developments. 4. Self assessment of: • working methods • increased knowledge • skill development 5. Formal assessment. Summative testing. 6. Peer group assessment of unusual salads. 7. Assessment of core skills.	**I.T.** Word processing CAD Charts/bar graphs Nutritional analysis **Literacy** Communication: • written • oral • visual **Numeracy** Costing Time management	Geography (countries of origin) Biology (physiology - NSP) Art (label design) Business studies (product development and marketing)

Fruit and vegetables

Planned activities

Teaching matrix 1 Questions

Total - 60 marks

1. Salad components are often pre-packaged ready for use. Name a pre-packaged product which you could buy in each of the following areas of the supermarket:
   - fruit section **(1)**
   - vegetable section. **(1)** **(2 marks)**

2. Salad bars are a feature of some supermarkets and fast food outlets. Comment on the components in the following selection choices:
   - Choice A - potato salad, coleslaw, mushrooms in vinaigrette, pasta salad, thousand island dressing **(3)**
   - Choice B - lettuce, tomatoes, melon wedge, sweetcorn, tomatoes, grated carrot. **(3)** **(6 marks)**

3. Compare the advantages and disadvantages of buying:
   a) a whole iceberg lettuce
   b) a bag of ready prepared salad leaves. **(4 marks)**

4. State two important factors which manufacturers have to consider when preparing vegetables for stir-fry packs. **(4 marks)**

5. Name a selection of vegetables, which could be included in a stir-fry pack. **(6 marks)**

6. Why do food manufacturers consider children to be a useful target market when developing new vegetable products? **(3 marks)**

7. What three methods of cooking are generally suggested for processed potato products? **(3 marks)**

8. List a range of qualities which consumers may look for in a ready prepared chip. **(4 marks)**

9. You have been given the brief to create a 'salad in a tub' with a mayonnaise or vinaigrette dressing. You want to make this a 'complete' lunch time snack suitable for office workers. State how you will incorporate components containing protein, carbohydrate, vitamin C, NSP and fat in your specification. **(10 marks)**

10. You are considering planning the menu for a buffet style vegetarian restaurant, and have made the following decisions:
    - the food selection will cater for vegans and lacto-vegetarians
    - there will be a variety of English dishes and others from around the world
    - there will be a range of desserts and a choice of two soups.

    a) How will you make sure customers know that dishes are appropriate for vegans? **(1)**
    b) How will you ensure the soup is served appropriately? **(3)**
    c) How will you inform people about the contents of the dishes? **(2)**
    d) What factors will you need to consider when replenishing dishes on the buffet? **(3)**
    e) How will you manage portion control? **(3)**
    f) How will you encourage and promote your reputation as a quality vegetarian restaurant with a family atmosphere? **(6)**

    (18 marks)

Planned activities

Fruit and vegetables

> ### Teaching matrix 1
> ### Answers

1. Suggestions might include:
fruit section - prepared fruits, e.g. pineapple, melon
vegetable section - varieties of salad leaves, carrot sticks, bean shoots.

2. Choice A:
- at least two dishes with mayonnaise - this will increase the fat content of the meal
- foods are generally softer in texture
- higher proportion of carbohydrate.

Choice B:
- lower in kilocalories and fat
- more colourful
- variety of textures.

3. Suggestions might include:
Iceberg lettuce:
- may be cheaper
- better value for money
- less convenient as some preparation is required
- only one variety of leaf.

Ready prepared salad leaves:
- generally more expensive
- smaller quantity
- may be considered poorer value for money
- mixed bags will provide a variety of flavours and colours.

4. Suggestions might include:
- vegetables must be of similar size for even cooking
- soft vegetables which easily disintegrate on cooking or during storage should not be used
- some components may be more costly to include
- all components need to have a similar shelf life to prevent deterioration and cross-contamination.

5. Suggestions might include:
- carrot
- celery
- courgette
- spring onions
- bean sprouts
- water chestnuts
- peppers.

6. Suggestions might include:
- parents welcome new products which appeal to children
- children are susceptible to marketing which features children or familiar images such as cartoons
- manufacturers realise that children may influence parents to buy new products.

7.
- frying
- grilling
- oven baking
- some may be microwaved.

8. Suggestions might include:
- crispy
- consistent shape
- golden
- quick and easy to cook
- range of shapes and varieties
- low fat content.

9. Suggestions might include:
- protein - mixed pulses, diced chicken, crunchy bacon, tuna, cottage cheese, ham, anchovy.
- carbohydrate - pasta, rice, gnocchi, potato
- vitamin C - peppers, avocado, oranges
- NSP - raw fruits and vegetables
- fat - mayonnaise or vinaigrette dressing, cheese.

10. a) Clear labelling on each of the dishes.

b) Suggestions might include:
- use hot plate on buffet, or custom made soup cauldron which keeps soup at correct temperature
- have one of the soups served cold as an alternative - chilling would be required for this, either ice bowl or kept in fridge
- ensure garnishes for soups are suitable for vegans, e.g. using alternatives to cream and frying croutons in vegetable oils.

c) Suggestions might include:
- labels on foods themselves
- information in menu
- information on chalk boards on the walls.

d) Suggestions might include:
- buffet kept tidy and clean
- spilled foods immediately wiped up
- bowls kept tidy
- dishes replaced when empty as wastage can occur if they are replaced too soon - people will always serve themselves from the new bowl
- unpopular dishes monitored to avoid risk of long term storage in warm conditions which may cause bacterial growth.

e) Suggestions might include:
- offering an 'all you can eat' meal at a set price
- food served by a member of staff who has been trained in portion control
- where customers serve themselves mark out portions and supply appropriate serving equipment.

f) Suggestions might include:
- state that children are welcome
- offer reduced rates (or free meals) for children
- provide high chairs
- advertise widely, using promotions to gain customer interest for example, having theme nights, childrens parties or celebration evenings
- provide 'nibble' bowls of fruit, nuts or seeds on individual tables
- ask customers on arrival if they have been to the restaurant before in order to determine their loyalty and inform them about the system for serving themselves.

Yeast products — Planned activities

Yeast products — Teaching matrix 2

	Students' book reference	Learning outcomes	Suggested activities
Food focus Yeast products	page 13 page 44	Increased awareness of range of breads available. Increased awareness of the versatility of bread doughs.	1. Sandwich tasting using same filling with different breads. Compare flavour and texture. 2. Investigate breads from around the world. Compare colour, flavour and texture. 3. Compare the performance of different types of yeast.
Nutrient focus Carbohydrates Vitamin B Calcium NSP	pages 55-6 pages 27 and 28 pages 23-4	NSP content of bread. Value of vitamin B and calcium in the diet. The function of carbohydrate in the diet.	**Ideas for practicals** 1. Traditional shapes. 2. Plaited loaf. 3. Harvest loaf. 4. Burger buns. 5. Compare ready made pizzas in terms of proportion of topping to base. 6. Compare the proportions of fat in a basic dough and an enriched dough. 7. Compare domestic and commercial dough making methods. 8. Safety: Focus on ovens and equipment, e.g. dough hooks, food processors and mixers.
Skills, knowledge and understanding Working economically Ratio and proportion. Sensory analysis Use of equipment Safety Teamwork Industrial/commercial practice	Unit 27 Pages 65, 69 Unit 23 Unit 18 Unit 19 Unit 26 Unit 20 page 128	Development of manipulative skills making doughs. Increased confidence in the use of electrical equipment. Development of specific forming and shaping skills. Simulation of industrial production systems. Understanding of the effect of yeast as a raising agent.	

Planned activities — Yeast products

Design briefs	Assessment	Opportunities	Cross-curricular
1. Design and produce a range of bread rolls for sale in a local bakery. Working as teams simulate commercial practices where possible. 2. Design and make a burger bun suitable for freezing. 3. Prepare a yeast dough and design and make a variety of plaited breads. (Advice could be obtained from a local baker.) 4. Design a bun using an enriched bread dough which would appeal to hungry school children.	Teacher assessment of: 1. Response to written questions and written activities. 2. Response to verbal questioning. 3. Observation and assessment of working methods and skill developments. 4. Self assessment of: • working methods • increased knowledge • skill development 5. Formal assessment. Summative testing. 6. Peer group assessment of plaited breads.	**I.T.** Word processing Photo/computer Spreadsheets for comparisons Systems Production lines **Literacy** Communication: • written • oral • visual **Numeracy** Costing Time management	Geography (regional/international breads)

Yeast products

Teaching matrix 2 Questions

Total - 35 marks

1. Name four different types of bread, which could be used for sandwiches. (4 x ½) **(2 marks)**

2. Name a typical bread from each of the following countries.
   a) Italy (1)
   b) India (1)
   c) Greece (1)
   d) France. (1) **(4 marks)**

3. What four conditions does yeast require in order to grow and reproduce? **(4 marks)**

4. What gas does yeast give off during reproduction? **(1 mark)**

5. What term is given to breads which do not have a raising agent? **(1 mark)**

6. Why do some cultures like to wrap foods inside bread or use it as an eating tool? **(2 marks)**

7. Evaluate making bread dough using each of the following pieces of equipment:
   a) a tabletop mixer fitted with a dough hook (3)
   b) a food processor. (3) **(6 marks)**

8. Quality controls involved in the industrial preparation of doughnuts are listed below. State why each check is important.
   a) Using standard recipe for yeast dough. (2)
   b) Accurate weighing of dough portions after shaping. (2)
   c) Using the same proportion of jam in each doughnut. (2) **(6 marks)**

9. Part baked dough products are popular today.
   a) Evaluate their use to the consumer. (4)
   b) How are these products packaged to maintain freshness and prevent deterioration? (2) **(6 marks)**

10. Below is a traditional bread recipe. Suggest changes to the method and alternative components which could shorten the process and make it more convenient to make.

    Traditional method
    15g fresh yeast
    ½ pint warm milk
    450g strong plain flour
    5ml salt
    1 egg to glaze

    Dissolve yeast in milk, leave for 15 mins to go frothy.
    Add yeast mixture to flour and salt, beat well together.
    Place in a warm place for 1 hour until doubled in size.
    Knead by hand for ten minutes.
    Knead lightly and shape the dough.
    Cover and leave in a warm place for 30 minutes or until doubled in size.
    Glaze.
    Bake at 230°C for ten minutes then 200°C for 25 minutes. **(3 marks)**

Planned activities   **Yeast products**

Teaching matrix 2 Answers

1. Suggestions might include:
   - white
   - bloomer
   - long tin
   - sliced
   - cob
   - granary
   - wholemeal.

2. Suggestions might include:
   a) ciabatta
   b) naan
   c) pitta
   d) croissant.

3. - Warmth
   - moisture
   - food
   - time.

4. Carbon dioxide.

5. Unleavened.

6. In some cultures there is a preference for using the hands to eat. The bread forms a convenient package for containing the food, e.g. pitta bread pockets.

7. a) Suggestions might include:
   - saves time and energy
   - efficient at turning and kneading dough though it may need a little hand finishing before shaping
   - care must be taken to ensure the machine remains stable - it can rock
   - relatively large amounts of dough can be mixed at one time.

   b) Suggestions might include:
   - smaller bowl is less convenient
   - lid means that flour does not escape from the machine
   - less room in the bowl for efficient turning and kneading of the dough
   - blades tend to cut rather than stretch and extend the dough.

8. a) To ensure that consistency of quality is established and maintained.
   b) and c) To ensure that all doughnuts conform to specification and to avoid wastage and profit loss.

9. a) Suggestions might include:
   - useful alternative to homemade bread
   - more convenient yet gives flavour and aroma of home baked bread
   - can be stored in the freezer until required
   - useful for someone who is not confident about breadmaking
   - tends to be more expensive than baked breads.

   b) Products are available in modified atmosphere packages (see Unit 25 in students' book).

10. Suggested adaptions:
    - use quick acting dried yeast
    - combine yeast with dry ingredients, add liquid and combine and knead using mixer
    - prove mixture only once.

Burgers, meat and fish

Planned activities

Burgers, meat and fish — Teaching matrix 3

	Students' book reference	Learning outcomes	Suggested activities
Food focus Burgers, meat and fish	pages 2-5 pages 22-3	Understanding of which foods provide protein. Understanding of the value of protein in the diet.	1. Blind tasting of a range of burgers to identify personal preferences. 2. Disassembly of a breaded chicken product. 3. Investigate the popularity of shaped and formed meat and vegetable products and evaluate their usefulness in the diet. 4. Compare the fat content of a range of burger products. 5. Identify the protein content of a vegetable, fish and meat burger. Compare the results with the RNI for a teenager. 6. Investigate legislation which governs minimum meat requirements for burgers.
Nutrient focus Protein Fat	pages 25-6 page 71	Understanding of the function of fat in the diet. Awareness of the nutrient content of various burger products. Awareness of the composition of burger products.	
Skills, knowledge and understanding Risk assessment HACCP Recipe adaption Law Dietary Reference Values Presentation and finishing Disassembly Food hygiene and safety Manipulative skills	Unit 31 page 141 Unit 16 Unit 30 Unit 7 Unit 21 Unit 24 Units 9 and 19 Unit 18	Development of manipulative skills in forming and shaping. Ability to make informed decisions about burger selection. Awareness of potential risks when handling and cooking high risk products. Ability to implement safety and hygiene practices.	**Ideas for practicals** 1. Identify the critical control points in burger production. 2. Compare methods of burger production using a variety of shaping techniques, e.g. hand, press, pastry cutter. 3. Produce and finish a range of burgers using previously made buns.

Planned activities

Burger, meat and fish

Design briefs	Assessment	Opportunities	Cross-curricular
1. Design and produce a burger product aimed at a particular cultural group. 2. Using I.T. skills design either a pamphlet or a wall chart which informs employees in a burger factory about the potential hazards during burger production. Include points for action. 3. Design and carry out a market research test on burger shrinkage and value for money. 4. Design a magazine page layout with the headline: 'Burgers can be healthy'.	Teacher Assessment of: 1. Response to written questions and activities. 2. Response to verbal questioning. 3. Observation and assessment of working methods and skill developments. 4. Self assessment of: • working methods • increased knowledge • skill development. 5. Formal assessment. Summative testing. 6. Peer group assessment of magazine layout.	**I.T.** Word processing CAD Photo/computer Spreadsheets Systems Production lines **Literacy** Communication: • written • oral • visual **Numeracy** Costing Time management Weighing Measuring	Science (bacterial growth and infection) Technology (design and suitability of burger shapers).

Burgers, meat and fish   **Planned activities**

Teaching matrix 3 Questions

Total - 70 marks

1. Name four breaded chicken products. **(4 marks)**

2. List three components found in meat burgers. **(3 marks)**

3. How would you cook a burger to reduce the fat content? **(1 mark)**

4. Name two disadvantages of buying economy burgers. **(4 marks)**

5. a) What are the functions of protein in the diet? **(3)**
   b) What are the two main types of protein? **(2)**   **(5 marks)**

6. Explain the function of a binding agent in the production of burgers. **(1 mark)**

7. Suggest two different ways in which you can shape and form burgers in the home. **(2 marks)**

8. a) State four processed meat or fish products which could form part of a barbecue menu. **(4)**
   b) Give reasons for your choice of foods. **(4)**
   c) Suggest ways in which you could reduce the risk of cross-contamination when cooking these products on a barbecue. **(4)**
   d) Name a pathogenic bacteria which could contaminate these foods. **(1)**
   e) What could be the symptoms of food poisoning caused by this bacteria? **(2)**
   f) Name five high risk foods. **(5)**   **(20 marks)**

9. You are to manufacture a low fat meat burger.
   a) State the type and quality of meat which could be used. **(2)**
   b) Suggest other components which could be used to create bulk and enhance the texture and flavour of the food. **(2)**
   c) Suggest an acceptable product size. **(2)**
   d) What would be your target group for marketing purposes? **(1)**
   e) What are the nutritional requirements of the burger? **(3)**
   f) What are the critical control points in the manufacture of the burger and what controls should be put in place to avoid hazards occuring? **(5)**   **(15 marks)**

10. List and discuss the criteria which could be used by the management of a fish restaurant in a sea side town when selecting dishes for their menu. They wish to appeal to a wide clientele including families with small children.   **(15 marks)**

Planned activities **Burgers, meat and fish**

Teaching matrix 3 Answers

1. Suggestions might include:
- Power Rangers
- Chicken Teddies
- Nuggets
- Chicken Kiev
- Chicken Cordon Bleu.

2. Suggestions might include:
meat, bread, onion, rusk, egg, flavourings.

3. Grill or barbecue.

4. Suggestions might include:
- may have a higher fat content
- may have a poorer flavour
- may shrink on cooking
- may have a high rusk content.

5. a) Growth and repair of body tissue, energy.
   b) High biological value - HBV (animal sources, soya).
   Low biological value - LBV (vegetable sources).

6. Binding agents such as egg hold the components together and help create a uniform shape.

7. Suggestions might include:
- burger press
- pastry cutter
- shaping by hand.

8. a) Suggestions might include:
- beefburger
- vegeburgers
- fish cakes
- lamb and beef grill steaks
- bacon burgers
- sausages.

   b) Suggestions might include:
- quick cooking food
- individually portioned
- include a variety of flavours
- include foods which are acceptable to different cultural or moral tastes
- cost.

   c) Suggestions might include:
- use separate serving dishes and tongs
- avoid handling raw and cooked foods
- keep raw and cooked food separate
- avoid contamination from raw marinades on cooked food.

   d) Suggestions might include:
- Salmonella
- Clostridium perfringens
- Staphylococcus aureus
- Escherichia coli (E-coli)
- Campylobacter jejuni.

   e) Symptoms of food poisoning:
- Salmonella - fever, headaches, diarrhoea, vomiting
- Clostridium perfringens - abdominal pain, diarrhoea
- Staphylococcus aureus - vomiting, abdominal pain, diarrhoea
- Escherichia coli (E-coli) - nausea, abdominal pain, diarrhoea
- Campylobacter jejuni - diarrhoea, flu-like symptoms.

   f) Suggestions might include:
- cooked meat
- cooked poultry
- shellfish and seafood
- gravies, sauces and stocks (marinades)
- egg products (binding agents)

9. a) Types of meat might include:
beef, pork, chicken, turkey, lamb, venison, ostrich.
Quality is determined by the ratio of meat to other components and the cut of meat used, e.g. fillet of beef versus beef flank and the age of the animal.

   b) Other components could be:
bread, rusk, onion, herbs, spices, garlic.

   c) Traditional burger weights are 50g standard, 100g large.

   d) Possibilities for target groups could be:
- children
- teenagers
- consumers of a speciality barbecue product
- consumers of a snack food.

   e) The product should supply:
- protein for growth and repair
- fat for warmth
- carbohydrates for energy.
The fat content should be closely monitored so that it compares favourably with other similar products on the market. This will affect the type and cut of meat chosen.

   f) Critical control points could include:
- slaughter (check for high standards)
- transportation (regulate temperature)
- storage at the food manufacturer (regulate temperature)
- butchery (ensure hygienic conditions)
- using machinery (avoid cross-contamination)
- food handling (staff hygiene training)
- packaging and transportation (regulate temperature).

10. Criteria could include:
- having a wide price range
- including some popular and familiar dishes
- including dishes which appeal to small children
- using more unusual fish, e.g. golden trout, ray, swordfish, shark.
- including a range of cooking methods
- setting high standards of hygiene throughout the restaurant
- using local produce.
- using fish in season with accompanying changing menu.

Chilled products **Plannned acivities**

Chilled products/Eggs and dairy food — Teaching matrix 4

	Students' book reference	Learning outcomes	Suggested activities
Food focus Chilled products Eggs and dairy foods	pages 47-8 pages 5-6 Unit 2	Awareness of the range of chilled and frozen products available. Understanding of the value of eggs and dairy foods in the diet.	1. Make recommendations to a pregnant woman regarding chilled products. 2. Investigate a range of cream and cream substitutes with special reference to whipping ability. 3. Analyse the effect of artificial colourings on a selection of same flavour yogurts. 4. Evaluate the properties of cream substitutes, e.g. fromage frais, crème fraîche, confectioners, custard. 5. Explain the function of setting agents within a chilled product. Consider mousses, trifles, yogurts and cheesecakes. 6. Investigate the variety of chilled desserts marketed for children. Analyse their nutrient content. 7. Identify the optimum storage times for a range of chilled desserts. 8. Compare the nutrient content of products which claim to be healthy with standard alternatives. 9. Compare and contrast different types of cheesecake with reference to basic components, cooked versus uncooked, filling and finishing.
Nutrient focus Additives Fats Carbohydrates	Unit 11 Unit 4 pages 20, 23-4	Awareness of the nutrient content of various products with special emphasis on: • sugar • fats • additives.	
Skills, knowledge and understanding Labelling Preservation Healthy eating Primary processing Working economically	pages 52, 108 Unit 10 Unit 12 pages 9-10 Unit 27	Increased understanding of marketing through label design. Awareness of information required on labels. Awareness of recipe adaption in order to make products at home more healthy. Understanding gels, emulsions and foams. Ability to make informed decisions regarding choice of product.	

Planned activities — Chilled products

Design briefs	Assessment	Opportunities	Cross-curricular
1. Design and produce a cheesecake for mass production. Consider accurate portion control in your design. 2. Design and produce a cream filled product suitable for a celebration. 3. Design a novel yogurt flavouring and its accompanying marketing campaign. 4. Design labels for: • a healthy yogurt for a child • a luxury dessert in a tub • an economy dessert.	Teacher assessment of: 1. Response to written questions and activities. 2. Response to verbal questioning. 3. Observation and assessment of working methods and skill developments. 4. Self assessment of: • working methods • increased knowledge • skill development. 5. Formal assessment. Summative testing. 6. Peer group assessment of magazine layout. 7. Assessment of core skills.	**I.T.** CAD Graphics for label design Spreadsheets **Literacy** Communication: • written • visual • oral **Numeracy** Portion control Measuring Proportion	Art (label design) Business studies and Media studies (marketing campaign) Maths (portion control)

Chilled products   **Planned activities**

Teacher matrix 4 Questions

Total - 45 marks

1. Name three chilled desserts found in supermarkets. (3 marks)

2. At what temperature should:
   a) domestic refrigerators (2)
   b) supermarket chillers (2)
   operate? (4 marks)

3. What type of cream would you use in the following:
   a) coffee (1)
   b) scones (1)
   c) soufflé (1)
   d) trifle? (1) (4 marks)

4. Give an advantage and a disadvantage of using aerosol cream. (2 marks)

5. What methods are used to preserve cream? (2 marks)

6. What products can act as setting agents in a dessert? (2 marks)

7. Suggest a vegetable alternative to gelatine. (1 mark)

8. State the uses of eggs in cookery. (6 marks)

9. Bio and very low fat are two different types of yogurt. Name four others. (4 marks)

10. Profiteroles, tiramisu, chocolate mousse and cheesecake are all popular chilled desserts.
    a) Account for their popularity amongst consumers. (3)
    b) What are the disadvantages of these products? (3)
    c) How could a cheesecake recipe be adapted to meet healthy eating guidelines? (3)
    d) Identify two different skills required when making each of these products. (8) (17 marks)

Planned activities **Chilled products**

Teaching matrix 4 Answers

1. Suggestions might include:
   - trifle
   - chocolate desserts
   - mousses
   - tiramisu
   - lemon meringue pie.

2. a) Domestic refrigerators - 1-4°C
   b) Chilled units in supermarkets - 1-8°C (though units housing cook chill products should operate at 0-3°C).

3. Suggestions might include:
   - coffee - single or half cream
   - scones - clotted or whipped double
   - soufflé - double
   - trifle - double or whipping.

4. Suggestions might include:
   ADVANTAGE
   - quick and easy to use
   - low fat varieties available
   - long shelf life
   DISADVANTAGE
   - collapses rapidly
   - more expensive.

5. UHT or freezing.

6. Suggestions might include:
   - gelatine
   - cornflour
   - eggs
   - arrowroot.

7. Suggestions might include:
   - agar agar
   - arrowroot
   - vegetarian gelatine substitute.

8. The uses of eggs in cookery are:
   - binding
   - glazing
   - enriching
   - aerating
   - garnishing
   - coating
   - as a main ingredient.

9. Types of yogurt could include:
   - very low fat
   - low fat
   - whole milk
   - creamy
   - Greek style
   - Bio.

10. a) Suggestions might include:
    - increased familiarity with foreign products due to holidays abroad
    - wide use as desserts on restaurant menus
    - high profile advertising
    - wide availability
    - large choice
    - reasonably inexpensive.

    b) Suggestions might include:
    - high sugar and fat content (saturated fat)
    - small portions
    - may have artificial flavour
    - heavily packaged therefore not environmentally friendly.

    c) Suggestions might include:
    - use cottage cheese
    - use half fat cream
    - use reduced fat biscuits
    - use low fat margarine
    - reduce the proportion of sugar in the recipe
    - increase the proportion of fresh fruit.

    d) Suggestions might include:
    - profiteroles - choux pastry, piping
    - tiramisu - custard, presentation skills
    - chocolate mousse - melting, whisking
    - cheesecake - biscuit base, use of gelatine.

Alternatives to meat and fish

Planned activities

Alternatives to meat and fish — Teaching matrix 5

	Students' book reference	Learning outcomes	Suggested activities
Food focus Alternatives to meat and fish	pages 23, 30, 103	Awareness of alternative protein sources. Increased awareness of the relative characteristics of different breads and their ability to contain a filling. Development of skills in sensory analysis.	1. Compare the merits of baguettes, pitta bread, bagels, croissants, baps and crispbreads as sandwich bases for a cheese or vegetable filling. 2. Visit an in-store bakery and investigate the range of regional and cultural breads produced. Research their popularity and say how they could be incorporated into a vegetarian diet. 3. Investigate a range of meatless sausages and carry out a consumer taste panel. 4. Investigate menus from fast food outlets. What provision do they make for non meat eaters? 5. Consumer questionnaire on meat eating habits. 6. Using the labels, compare the nutrients and components in a snack meal containing meat, e.g. lasagne or stir fry, and its vegetarian equivalents. Comment on the protein content, and the RNI for your age group. 7. Disassemble a range of non meat sandwiches with similar fillings from different outlets. Compare quantity and quality of fillings, nutritional value and value for money. 8. Research how either tofu or TVP is produced and display this process as a system. 9. Investigate a range of flavours which compensate for the blandness of meatless products. 10. Investigate a range of recipes using nuts and seeds.
Nutrient focus NSP Protein Vitamins B12, B1 Iodine	page 55 pages 2 and 103 pages 27, 29	Development of skills in analysis with regard to cost, nutrition and palatability.	
Skills, knowledge and understanding Packaging Disassembly Systems Secondary processing Meal planning Storage Special diets	Unit 25 Unit 24 Unit 28 pages 62-3 Unit 8 pages 2-3, 4, 6, 9, 10, 13, 14, 15 Unit 13	Development of research skills in industrial production methods. Development of skills in weighing and measuring. Development of decision making skills in factors affecting consumer choice and product availability. Development of skills in product evaluation. Understanding of reasons for special diets.	

Planned activities — Alternatives to meat and fish

Design briefs	Assessment	Opportunities	Cross-curricular
1. Design and market a range of sandwich products which would sell well in your school. Suggest a range of flavours and fillings which would appeal to different cultures. 2. The English sandwich has become the fashionable snack to eat in France. Design a variety of fillings and suggest breads which could be interpreted as typically English. Design a production and transportation system for these sandwiches. 3. Design and produce a ready meal product which is acceptable to non meat eating consumers. 4. Design, cost and package a healthy sandwich based on knowledge gained from disassembly. 5. Design a new range of lasagnes using vegetables and meat alternatives. 6. Explore the potential of tofu and Quorn. 7. Design and produce a recipe booklet to include recipes which can be cooked in 10, 20 or 40 minutes. Focus on dishes using nuts, pulses, vegetables and meat substitutes.	Teacher assessment of: 1. Response to written questions and activities. 2. Response to verbal questioning. 3. Observation and assessment of working methods and skill developments. 4. Self assessment of: • working methods • increased knowledge • skill development. 5. Formal assessment. Summative testing. 6. Peer group assessment of sensory analysis. 7. Assessment of core skills.	**I.T.** Word processing Spreadsheets Systems Production lines Data analysis Nutritional analysis **Literacy** Communication: • written • oral • visual **Numeracy** Weighing Measuring Timing	Geography (eating habits of different cultures) Business studies (costings, product development and marketing)

Alternatives to meat and fish   **Planned activities**

Teaching matrix 5 Questions

Total - 70 marks

1. What is the difference between a lacto-vegetarian and a vegan?   **(2 marks)**

2. Suggest reasons why people choose to be vegetarians.   **(2 marks)**

3. Sort the following foods into these groups:
   a) Suitable for lacto vegetarians. **(3)**
   b) Suitable for vegans. **(3)**
   c) Suitable for non-vegetarians. **(3)**   **(9 marks)**

butter	cheese	Quorn	chicken	tofu
suet pastry	cream	Marmite	soya beans	Bovril
strawberry mousse (made with gelatine)		fish	mayonnaise	

4. a) What is the function of iodine in the diet? **(1)**
   b) What disease can be caused by a deficiency of iodine? **(1)**   **(2 marks)**

5. Suggest dishes produced by a fast food outlet which may be suitable for vegetarians.   **(3 marks)**

6. List four sandwich fillings suitable for a lacto-vegetarian.   **(4 marks)**

7. Explain what the following foods are made from:
   a) Quorn **(2)**
   b) tofu. **(2)**   **(4 marks)**

8. What nutrients might vegetarians lack in their diet? How could they ensure that they do not become deficient in these nutrients?
                                                                                                                                                (9 marks)

9. Eating habits with regard to meat eating have changed over the years.
   a) What factors have influenced these changes? **(4)**
   b) Plan three vegetarian menus suitable for the following situations:
- a packed lunch
- a snack lunch
- a cooked lunch. **(9)**
   Indicate how you have ensured adequate provision of protein, iron and vitamin C.
   c) Account for the change in numbers of people preferring white to red meat. **(4)**   **(17 marks)**

10. Many people choose to eat fish as an alternative to meat. As a result, the market in canned fish products has expanded.
    a) Canned fish can be bought in oil, brine, tomato sauce and mayonnaise.
    Evaluate the use of each of these products. **(8)**
    b) Name a dish in which each of the following canned fish products can be used:
- sardines
- tuna
- salmon
- mackerel
- pilchards. **(10)**   **(18 marks)**

Planned activities **Alternatives to meat and fish**

Teaching matrix 5 Answers

1. A lacto-vegetarian eats dairy products; a vegan will not eat any food derived from an animal source.

2. Suggestions might include:
   - dislike the thought of killing animals for food
   - do not like the taste of meat
   - religious requirements
   - health reasons.

3. Lacto-vegetarian - cheese, Quorn, tofu, cream, Marmite, soya beans, mayonnaise, butter.
   Vegan - Quorn, tofu, Marmite, soya beans.
   Non-vegetarian - all foods.

4. a) Iodine regulates the metabolic rate.
   b) Goitre.

5. Suggestions might include:
   - egg McMuffin
   - bean burgers
   - vegetable burger
   - pizza
   - salads.

6. Suggestions might include:
   - cheese
   - peanut butter
   - marmite
   - salad.

7. a) Quorn is made from a mushroom type fungi, it is also referred to as mycoprotein.
   b) Tofu is made from soya milk curd produced when soya milk is mixed with calcium sulphate then pressed and drained.

8. Suggestions might include:
   - vitamin B12 which can be supplied by milk, eggs, fortified breakfast cereals or supplements
   - iron which can be supplied by pulses, cereals, egg yolk and green vegetables (vitamin C should be eaten with iron to aid absorption)
   - protein which can be supplied by eggs, dairy products or complementary vegetable proteins, e.g. bread and beans.

9. a) Suggestions might include:
   - more health awareness
   - more readily available vegetarian alternatives
   - more vegetarian restaurants
   - influence of BSE
   - moral issues.
   b) Any reasonable answer. Suggestions might include:
   - packed lunch - quiche with watercress and orange salad, selection of dried fruits
   - snack lunch - jacket potato with cheese and beans, fresh fruit
   - cooked lunch - vegetable lasagne or curry, chocolate and orange mousse.

   Iron provided by watercress, chocolate, curry and dried fruit. Protein provided by quiche, cheese, beans, mousse, pasta and vegetables. Vitamin C provided by orange, potato and fresh fruit.

   c) Suggestions might include:
   - more health awareness - less saturated fat in white meat
   - quick and convenient to cook
   - large availability of white meat products both fresh and processed
   - lower in kilocalories
   - reasonable inexpensive
   - influence of BSE.

10. a) Suggestions might include:
    oil - keeps the product moist, adds vitamins A and D to the product, has a good flavour, the traditional canning liquor for sardines, salmon, etc.
    brine - lowers fat content of the product
    tomato sauce - increases the variety of the product, adds flavour to the basic product and can be used as the basis for other dishes, e.g. on a pizza
    mayonnaise - allows the product to be easily incorporated into salads, saves time in having to blend the components yourself, high in fat.
    b) Any acceptable answer, suggestions might include:
    - tuna salad niçoise
    - tuna and pasta bake
    - pilchard salad
    - salmon filo parcels
    - mackerel paté
    - sardine pizza.

New products   **Planned activities**

New product development/Food as a material   Teaching matrix 6

	Students' book reference	Learning outcomes	Suggested activities

Food focus
 	
New product development
 	
Food as a material
	Unit 22
	
	Unit 14
		Awareness of:
		• the development during the past five years of ready made and convenience foods
		• how foods can be adapted to suit the needs of a particular consumer group
		• the range of:
		   ready made dressings available
		   yogurts available.
			1. Investigate the range of ready made dressings which could accompany salads.
			2. Analyse the statement 'fitness for purpose' in relation to yogurts for children, teenagers and speciality yogurts.
			3. Compile a day's menu for four people. Identify any components used which are the result of product development during the past five years. Comment on the nutritional content of these particular components. If possible compare with their earlier alternatives.
			4. Select three same flavour cook-in sauces and carry out a blind tasting to determine flavour preference.
			5. Evaluate the developments which have taken place in pastry production.
			6. Evaluate the quality of bought components compared with home made equivalents, e.g. frozen Yorkshire puddings, ready made custards, shaker cakes.
			7. Make recommendations to someone who wishes to try dishes from around the world.
			Focus on:
			• Indian
			• Thai
			• Chinese
			• Italian
			• Mexican.
			8. Investigate the range of packaging materials employed in the sale of salads and/or vegetables.

Nutrient focus Healthy eating in processed products	Unit 12 page 60	Awareness of the nutritional content of processed products and how processing may affect nutritional content. Understanding of current dietary targets. Consideration of how consumer choice and food production and processing methods may affect the achievement of these targets.	
Skills, knowledge and understanding Quality Production methods Industrial applications Additives Preservation Storage Manipulative skills Proportions Presentation Packaging	Unit 29 Unit 22 page 128 Unit 28 page 121 Unit 11 page 53 Unit 10 pages 2-3, 4, 6, 9, 10, 13, 14, 15 Unit 18 pages 65-6 Unit 21 Unit 25	Development of manipulative skills with particular reference to: • pastry making skills • forming and shaping. Understanding of the range of packaging materials available. Continued development of sensory analysis skills. Understanding of the developing range of multicultural products. Understanding of the processes involved in the development of new products. Understanding of how advertising affects consumer choice. Presentation of results.	

Planned activities

New products

Design briefs	Assessment	Opportunities	Cross-curricular
1. Design a menu using a range of components which have undergone secondary processing. 2. Design a menu which incorporates a range of ready made products suitable for a childrens' party or adult celebration. Carry out a cost and time comparison with traditional production methods. 3. Select a product from the supermarket and design an advertising campaign which promotes it to an identified target group. Work either on your own or in a group. Present your findings to a larger audience, using appropriate I.T. techniques. 4. Identify a selection of recipes which make use of the wide variety of stock cubes and dried flavourings now available. Produce one dish. Photograph and evaluate your results. Collate your ideas into a simple recipe booklet.	Teacher Assessment of:- 1. Response to written questions and activities. 2. Response to verbal questioning. 3. Observation and assessment of working methods and skill developments. 4. Self assessment of: • working methods • increased knowledge • skill development. 5. Formal assessment. Summative testing. 6. Peer group assessment of magazine layout. 7. Assessment of core skills. 8. Assessment of presentation results.	**I.T.** Word processing DTP Spreadsheets for comparisons Systems Production lines Graphics for presentation **Literacy** Communication: • written • oral • visual **Numeracy** Nutritional data analysis	Art (booklet design) Geography (transport systems, countries/location)

New products — **Planned activities**

Teaching matrix 6 Questions

Total - 50 marks

1. Give an example of a dish from India, China and Thailand. (3 marks)

2. What is meant by market research? (2 marks)

3. What is a target group? (1 mark)

4. What does 'fitness for purpose' mean? (2 marks)

5. What is a prototype? (2 marks)

6. a) Name the four main groups of additives. **(4)**
   b) Which law controls their use? **(1)** (5 marks)

7. A mini quiche to be sold chilled is in its prototype stage. The company's aim is to produce a product which satisfies guidelines for healthy eating.
   a) What are the main stages in the development of the quiche? **(8)**
   b) Suggest five questions you might ask tasters before deciding on your final product size and recipe. **(5)** (13 marks)

8. Salads and vegetables are packaged in a variety of ways to ensure freshness and protection. What factors would be considered when deciding upon the type of packaging used? (6 marks)

9. a) What is modified atmosphere packaging? **(1)**
   b) What are the advantages of using modified atmosphere packaging? **(2)**
   c) Give three examples of products packaged in this way. **(3)** (6 marks)

10. a) What is quality control? **(2)**
    b) Write a paragraph which explains the value of an effective quality control system for a food processing company. **(8)** (10 marks)

Planned activities

New products

Teaching matrix 6 Answers

1. Any reasonable answer. Suggestions might include:
- India - dhal
- China - vegetable stir fry
- Thailand - green curry.

2. The collection, analysis and interpretation of information about the consumption of goods and services.

3. The intended users of a product.

4. A product is 'fit for its purpose' when it is correctly targeted towards and suitable for a particular consumer group, e.g. yogurt for children.

5. A sample of a product, including its packaging, made during the design stage.

6. a) Colours, preservatives, antioxidants, emulsifiers/stabilisers.
   b) Food Act 1984.

7. a) The main stages in the development of the quiche could be:
- initial brief
- market research
- generation of ideas
- product specification
- product modification
- first production run
- test marketing
- product launch.

b) Any appropriate answers which relate to sensory appeal, for example:
- texture of pastry
- size of filling components
- overall size
- visual appeal
- aroma
- texture and flavour of filling.

8. Suggestions might include:
- fragility of the product
- importance of product visibility
- weight
- cost
- recyclability
- ease of use
- product's rate of decay.

9. a) The product is packaged in a plastic bag in which oxygen, carbon dioxide and nitrogen have been pumped. It is then hermetically sealed.
   b) Suggestions might include:
- the food is packaged in peak condition
- the shelf life of the product is extended
- colour deterioration is reduced.
   c) Suggestions might include:
- salads
- fresh pasta
- sliced bacon
- meat/fish
- part baked dough products
- poppadoms.

10. a) Quality control is a way of checking the quality of a product during and/or at the end of a production system.
    b) The value of quality control is to set and maintain standards within the production process. This is important as consumers will demonstrate loyalty to a company who can guarantee a standardised product which conforms to customers' expectations. This, in turn, will provide profits for the company.

Section 3

Reference material

This section provides a series of photocopiable pro formas, including guides, charts and tables. The pro formas have been divided into six sections:
- research sheets
- technology process sheets
- practical planners
- planning sheets
- data analysis sheets
- blank charts and guides.

Here are some suggestions for how you could use the pro formas.

1. Research sheets

p. 110 Questionnaire
- Questionnaire to record data for consumer research.
- Questions result in sub-divided answers.
- At the bottom of the page students can analyse their data to form conclusions.

p. 111 Questionnaire
- Example of how questionnaire could be used.
- This pro forma can be used with the activity on p. 3 of the students' book.

pp. 112 and 113 Comparison sheets
- Allow students to collate data from comparative studies, for example, taste testing and food trials.
- These sheets may be used in conjunction with the ruled lines sheet on p. 139.

2. Technology process sheets

p. 114 Product specification
- Provides students with a structure for product analysis.
- May be used as a planning tool for an intended practical.
- May be used as part of a disassembly process.

p. 115 Evaluating existing products
- Assists in the analysis of target groups.
- Allows students to compare similar products.

p. 116 Recipe development and evaluation
- State recipe and source.
- Record method of preparation.
- After practical activity students evaluate the performance of the components.
- Analysis may include: organoleptic properties, nutritional content, presentation and suitability of purpose. It may also involve the preparation and cooking method.
- Students can then suggest any necessary adaptions to the original recipe components and methods.

p. 117 Organisation and management
- Allows for action planning and monitoring of individual tasks, design brief or set of tasks.
- Allows both students and teachers to monitor and record progress.

p. 118 Hygiene and safety procedures
- Checklist of tasks to be carried out before practical.
- Evaluation of hygiene and safety procedures after practical.

p. 119 Evaluation help sheet 1
- Helps evaluation by prompting the students through the process.
- More able students will be able to expand their answers.

p. 120-1 Evaluation help sheet 2 (2 pages)
- An ongoing evaluation enabling students to record comments at each stage.

3. Practical planners

p. 122 Shopping order
- A shopping list.
- Allows students to classify the components needed for practical activities.
- Facilitates organised shopping.

p. 123 Recipe planner
- A compact method of recording each stage of the recipe.

p. 124 Costing sheet
- Helps students to cost each dish.

4. Planning sheets

p. 125 Visual design planner 1
- A visual way of presenting initial design ideas.
- Circles can be used to draw designs, e.g. cakes, pizzas, pies etc.
- Boxes can be used to suggest a name (top box), and individual variations and flavourings underneath.

p. 126 Visual design planner 2
- Allows space for drawing top and cross-sectional views.
- Gives an overview of the practical activity.

p. 127 Design planner
- Centre oval may contain illustration of finished product.
- Boxes may contain variation possibilities.
- Bottom rectangle can contain criteria for choice.

Reference material

5. Data analysis sheets

p. 128 **Table**
- Checklist to enable students to compare products.

p. 129 **Nutrition information chart**
- A means of recording nutritional data.
- Can be used for products or dietary analysis.
- Other nutrients can be added to table.

p. 130 **Food facts**
- Allows students to produce concise information about specific commodities.
- Can be used for module work or for revision purposes.

6. Blank charts/and guides

p. 131 **Brainstorm chart (6 ideas)**
- Can be used whenever students are asked to brainstorm ideas (see Unit 26).

p. 132 **Brainstorm chart (10 ideas)**
- Can be used whenever students are asked to brainstorm ideas (see Unit 26).

p. 133 **Planning schedule**
- Can be used to plan sequence of work.

p. 134 **Flow chart**
- Basic flow chart with start and stop and process boxes (see Unit 26).
- Can be cut and pasted to correct size.

p. 123 **Pie chart**
- Can be used to create pie charts if software not available.

p. 136 **Menu blank**
- Can be used to create attractive menus.

p. 137 **Menu fonts**
- Different fonts for menu title.
- Can be used to cut and paste.

p. 138 **Lines - Portrait**
- Can be used under pro formas to enable students to write neatly and clearly.

p. 139 **Lines - Landscape**
- Can be used under pro formas to enable students to write neatly and clearly.

p. 140 **Key Stage 4 Design and Technology mapping pro forma**

Reference material

Questionnaire on _____

Name _____ Date _____

Group _____

Please would you answer the following questions as part of a survey on _____

Question _____

Yes _____	No _____
Yes _____	No _____
Yes _____	No _____
Yes _____	No _____
Yes _____	No _____
Yes _____	No _____

2. Question _____

Conclusions

Reference material

Questionnaire on meat eating	
Name_____	Date_____
Group_____	

Please would you answer the following questions as part of a survey on meat eating

1. In the last week have you eaten any the following meats?

Pork	Yes	_____	No	_____
Beef	Yes	_____	No	_____
Lamb	Yes	_____	No	_____
Chicken	Yes	_____	No	_____
Turkey	Yes	_____	No	_____
Burgers	Yes	_____	No	_____

2. State the cooking method used.

	Pork	**Beef**	**Lamb**	**Chicken**	**Turkey**	**Burgers**
Fried						
Grilled						
Roast						
Stewed						
Braised						

Conclusions

Reference material

Comparison of

Name _____

Group _____   Date _____

Preparation method	Ease of preparation	Texture	Flavour	Other comments

Conclusions

Reference material

Comparison of _____

Name _____
Group _____
Date _____

Product	Cost	Appearance	Colour	Texture	Flavour	No. of portions	Comments

Reference material

Product specification

Name_____ Date_____

Group_____

Product

Colour

Texture

Quantity

Cost

Appearance

Nutritive value

Recipe/Ingredients

Description of packaging

Reference material

Evaluating existing products

Name _____ **Date** _____

Group _____

Product [_____]

Description of product _____
_____
_____

Who would you eat this product? [_____]

List reasons why this product would appeal to the person(s) identified above?
_____
_____
_____

Product [_____]

Description of product _____
_____
_____

Who would you eat this product? [_____]

List reasons why this product would appeal to the person(s) identified above?
_____
_____

Reference material

Recipe development and evaluation
Name _____ Date _____
Group _____

Product/Recipe _____

Ingredients	Method

Evaluation

Recipe component	Analysis	Adaption

Reference material

Organisation and management of _____

Name _____ Date _____

Group _____

Checklist 1 **Completed**

Planning	Student	Teacher

Checklist 2 **Completed**

Making	Student	Teacher

Checklist 3 **Completed**

Evaluation	Student	Teacher

Reference material

Hygiene and safety procedures

Name _____   Date _____

Group _____

Check list	Yes	No
Before practical 1. Is all equipment clean? 2. Are you properly dressed for food preparation? 3. Are your hands clean? Do you need a plaster? 4. Is your work area properly organised for a fast, clean and safe practical?		

After practical
 	
5. Have you used the correct knives safely for the tasks tackled in the practical?
6. Have you left sharp implements in a bowl of soapy water at any time during the practical?
7. Have you touched your:
   face
   hair
   handkerchief
   without then washing your hands?
8. Have you used all large equipment safely and hygienically?
9. Has all equipment been cleaned and then both safely and neatly stored after use?
10. Has your completed dish passed all critical control points satisfactorily?		

Evaluation of practical

The areas where I worked well were _____

_____

The areas where I need to take more care are _____

_____

Staff Comments

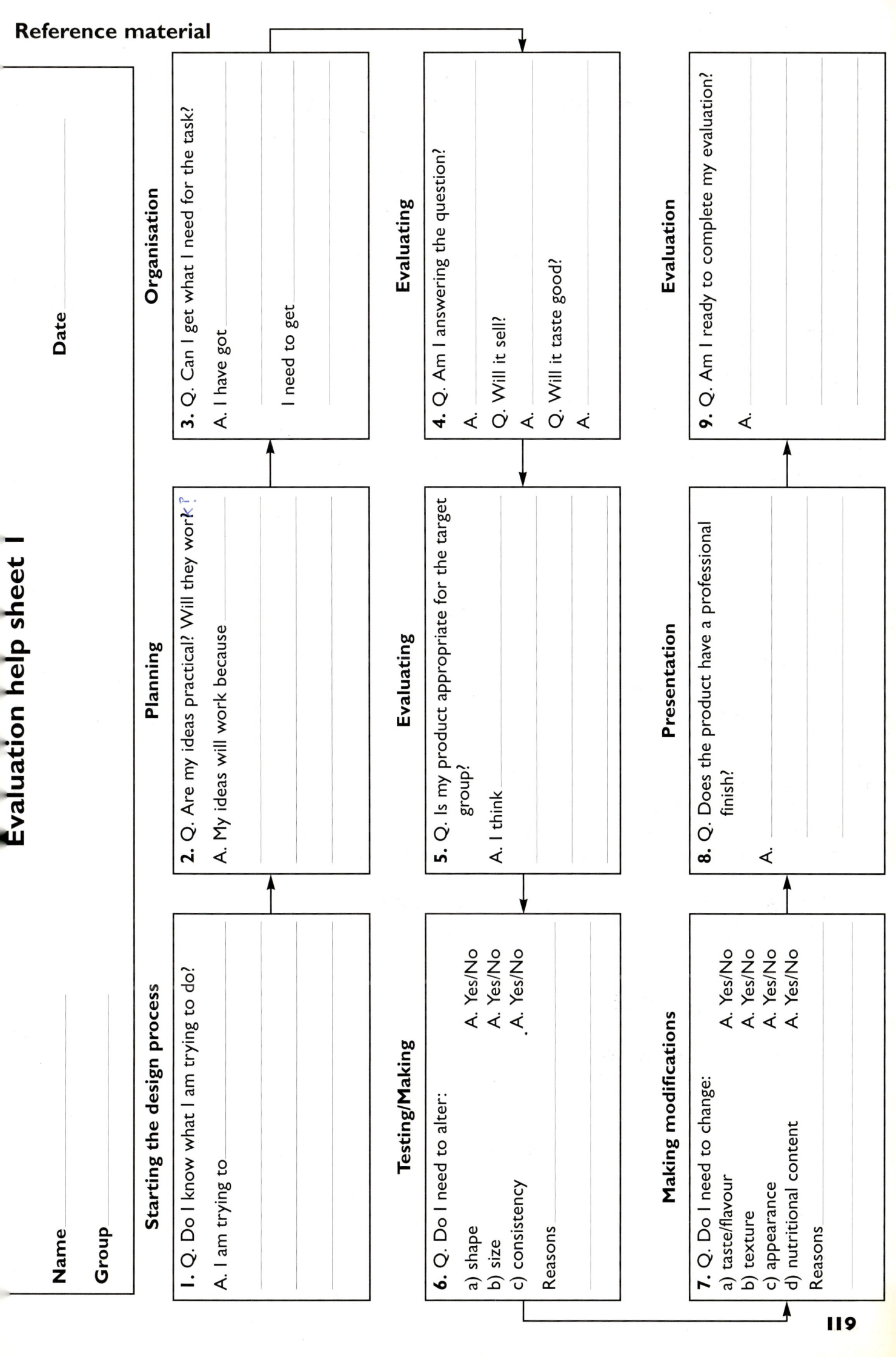

Evaluation help sheet 1

Reference material

Name _____
Group _____

Date _____

Starting the design process

1. Q. Do I know what I am trying to do?

A. I am trying to _____

Planning

2. Q. Are my ideas practical? Will they work?

A. My ideas will work because _____

Organisation

3. Q. Can I get what I need for the task?

A. I have got _____

I need to get _____

Evaluating

4. Q. Am I answering the question?

A. _____
Q. Will it sell?
A. _____
Q. Will it taste good?
A. _____

Evaluating

5. Q. Is my product appropriate for the target group?

A. I think _____

Testing/Making

6. Q. Do I need to alter:
a) shape   A. Yes/No
b) size   A. Yes/No
c) consistency A. Yes/No

Reasons _____

Making modifications

7. Q. Do I need to change:
a) taste/flavour   A. Yes/No
b) texture   A. Yes/No
c) appearance   A. Yes/No
d) nutritional content A. Yes/No

Reasons _____

Presentation

8. Q. Does the product have a professional finish?

A. _____

Evaluation

9. Q. Am I ready to complete my evaluation?

A. _____

119

Reference material

Evaluation help sheet 2

Name _____ **Date** _____

Group _____

Planning Notes should be added to this box after every lesson. They should include how the original plan was made, and any later changes, with reasons.

Organisation Notes should be made on the way work was organised, by whom, and how well your plans worked each week.

Reviewing This process should be continuous. Always go back and decide if anything could be changed to improve the work you are doing. Make notes so that you do not forget.

Reference material

Evaluation help sheet 2

Name_____   Date_____

Group_____

Making Keep a careful record of the organisation and management of any practical work. It is very important to show as many different practical skills as possible. You must work efficiently, quickly, safely and hygienically. A variety of equipment should be used throughout the task. You must understand the cooking processes used, e.g. the use of yeast and how it works.

Presentation This should include flavour, appearance, colour, texture and a uniform size if several are made. Photographs showing the development of the product throughout the project enhances the completed work.

Evaluating If you have kept your notes up to date throughout this activity, you should now be able to complete the final evaluation which analyses everything you have learned from this piece of work.

Finally... Work which includes use of information technology is very important and will help you with your final assessment.

Reference material

Shopping order

Name _____   Date _____

Group _____

Fish		Fruit		Vegetables	
Quantity	Item	Quantity	Item	Quantity	Item

Meat	
Quantity	Item

Supermarket			
Quantity	Item	Quantity	Item

Dishes to be made

Reference material

Recipe planner

Name _____   Date _____

Group _____

Name of dish			
Quality	Ingredient/food item	Quantity	Ingredient/food item

Equipment needed		Oven temperature & Cooking times

Recipe/Method/Order of work/Flow chart

1	
2	
3	
4	
5	
6	
7	
8	
9	
10	

Reference material

Costing sheet

Name _____   Date _____

Group _____

Name of dish

Amount	Ingredient	Price
	Total	

Name of dish

Amount	Ingredient	Price
	Total	

Reference material

Date

Name

Group

Visual design planner 1

Design brief

Visual design planner 2

Name	Date	Group	Flow chart of

Design of

Bird's eye view

List of ingredients
-
-
-
-
-
-
-
-
-
-

Cross-section

Cooking/storage

Reference material

Reference material

Date

Name

Group

Design planner

Design brief

127

Reference material

Table to show product varieties and target groups

Name _____ Date _____

Group _____

Product name/brand	Product description	Target group

Conclusions

Reference material

Nutrition information chart

Name _____   Date _____

Group _____

Nutrient			
Energy kcal kj			
Protein			

Carbohydrate
        Starch
        Sugar			

Fat			
Iron			
Vitamin A			
Vitamin B1 (thiamin)			
Vitamin C			
Vitamin D			
NSP			
Sodium			

Reference material

Food facts

Name_____ Date_____

Group_____

Variety/sources	Structure

	Nutritional value
Uses	

Special information

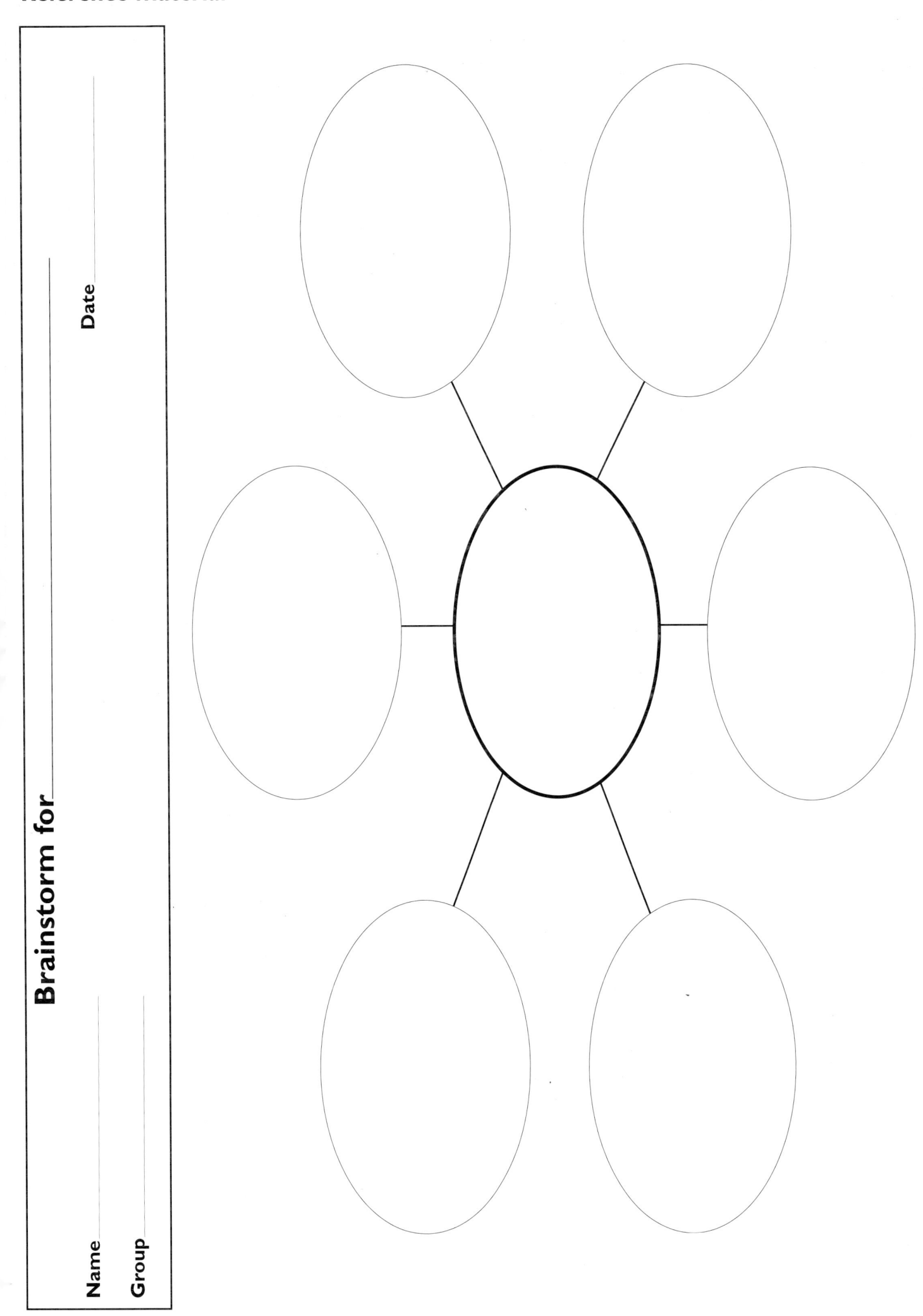

Reference material

Brainstorm for _____

Name _____
Group _____
Date _____

131

Brainstorm for _____

Name _____
Date _____
Group _____

Reference material

132

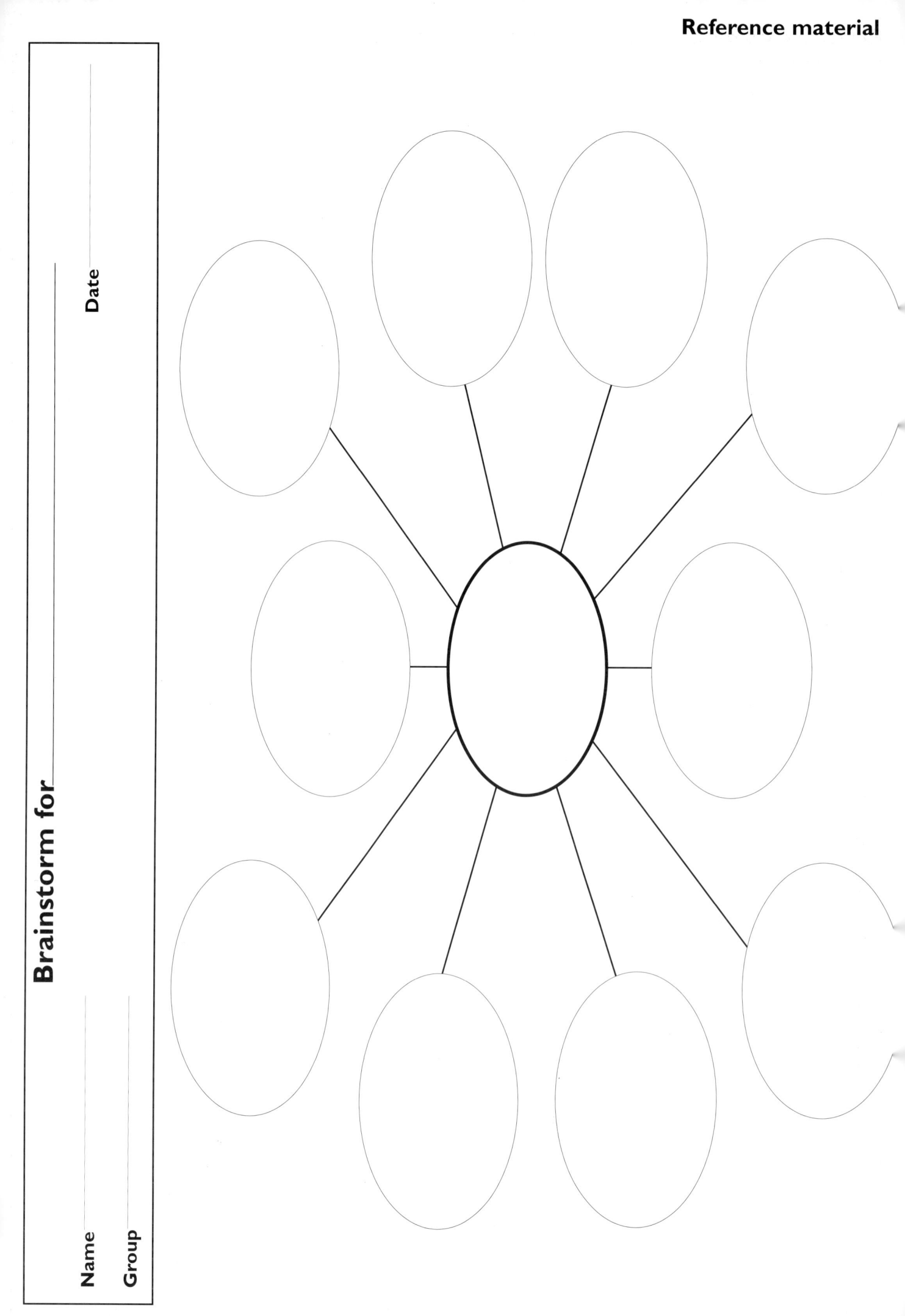

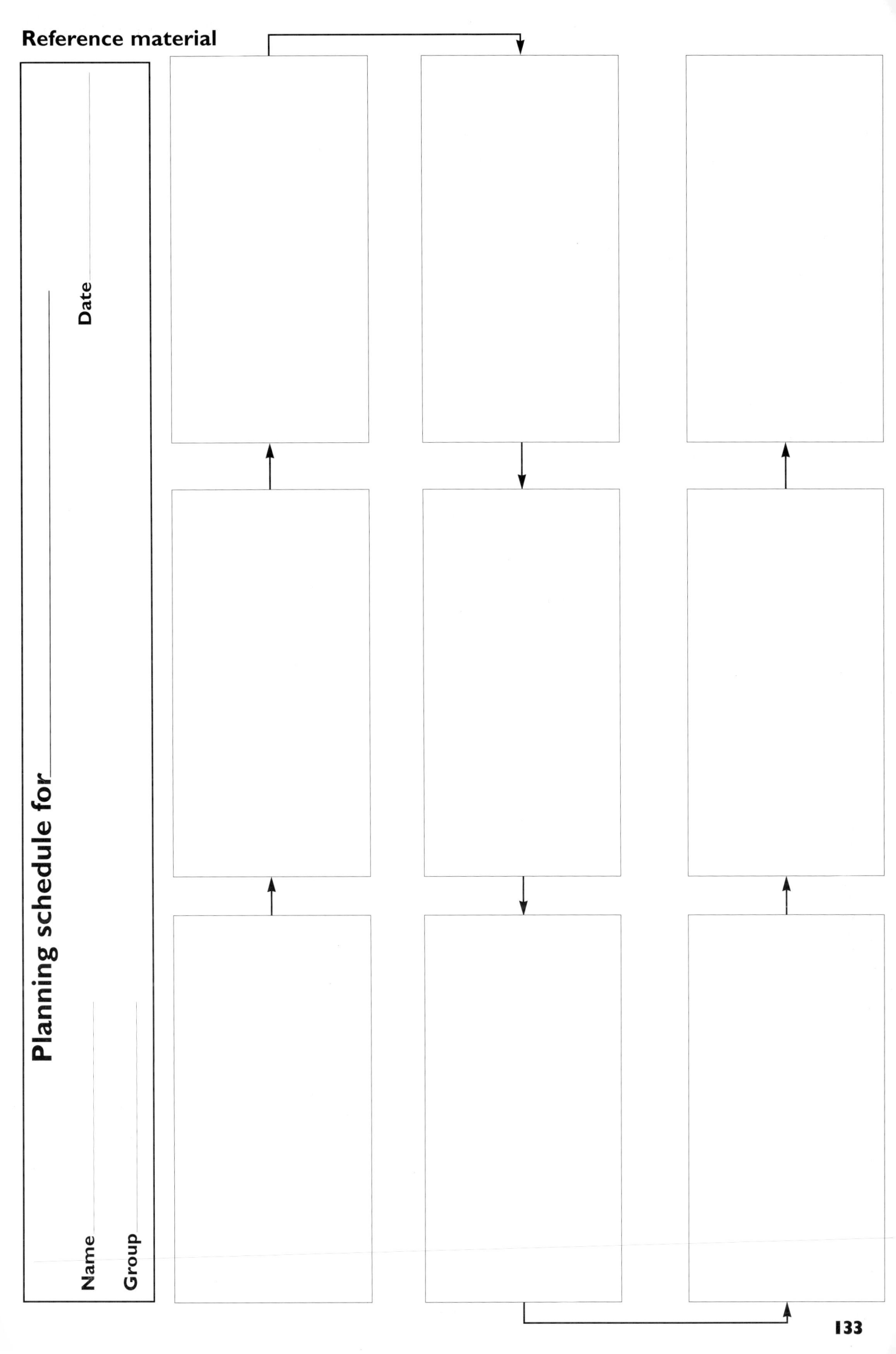

Reference material

Planning schedule for

Name
Group
Date

Reference material

Flow chart of _____

Name _____ **Date** _____

Group _____

Reference material

Pie chart

Name _____   **Date** _____

Group _____

135

Date	Group	Name

Reference material

MENU

Reference material

Date	Group	Name

Menu Menu

Menu *Menu*

Menu Menu

Menu Menu

Menu **Menu**

Menu Menu

Menu Menu

Reference material

Key Stage 4 Design and Technology mapping proforma

Reference material

KS4 Programmes of study	Matrix Nos.	1	2	3	4	5	6	7	8	9	10	11	12
1a. design & make assignments	1. Opportunities for capability through												
1b. focused practical tasks													
1c. investigate, disassemble & evaluate activities													
2a. apply PoS of other subjects	2. Opportunities to												
3a. develop & use design briefs	3. Designing skills												
3b. anticipate & design for product maintenance													
3c. design for manufacturing in quantity													
3d. recognise conflicting demands when designing													
3e. consider increasing range of users													
3f. determine degree of accuracy required for manufacture													
3g. generate designs against pre-set criteria & modify where necessary													
3h. use of I.T. in design modelling & decision making													
3i. produce & use detailed schedules to achieve objective with alternatives													
3j. be flexible & able to respond to changes & opportunities													
3k. devise & apply procedures to test for quality at critical control points													
3l. ensure product quality suitable for intended users													
4a. match materials, components with tools equipment & processes													
4b. use equipment appropriately to achieve a finish matching product specification													
4c. use industrial applications for familiar materials & processes													
4d. know the difference between quality control & quality assurance techniques													
4e. know how products are manufactured in quantity using the above													
4f. know how CAM is used in manufacturing in quantity, single items & batches													
4g. to simulate production & assembly lines													
4h. produce & use detailed working schedules, including deadlines & CCPs													
4i. evaluate quality of products & devise modifications to improve performance													
4j. be adaptable in working practices & respond to changes													
4k. devise & apply procedures to test for quality at critical control points													
4l. test, modify & evaluate suitability for intended user	4. Making skills												
5a. how materials are cut shaped & formed to designated tolerances													
5b. how materials are combined creating useful properties then utilised in industry													
5c. how materials are prepared for manufacture, allowing for waste & fine finishing													
5d. self finishing & applied finishing processes appreciating aesthetics & function													
5e. relationship between component & intended purpose													
5f. the use of pre-manufactured standard components to improve performance	5. Materials & components												
6a. how control systems & sub-systems are designed to achieve different purposes													
6b. how to incorporate feedback within their own systems													
6c. how to analyse the performance of systems	6. Systems & control												
7a. intended purpose of the product	7. Products & applications												
7b. components available for use in the product													
7c. choice of materials & ways they have been used													
7d. the processes used to produce them													
7e. the application of scientific principles													
7f. the market for which the product is intended													
7g. the range of alternative products & solutions													
8a. how far it meets a clear need	8. Quality												
8b. its fitness for purpose													
8c. whether it is an appropriate use of resources													
8d. its impact beyond the purpose for which it was designed													
8e. how far it meets manufacturability & maintenance requirements													
9a. take responsibility for recognising hazards	9. Health & safety												
9b. use information sources to assess risk of the unfamiliar													
9c. manage environment & justify the action to control the risk													

Section 4

Product and business index

Page numbers in **bold** show where a word is included in an activity or Case Study.

A
aduki beans 13
Advanced Hygienic Walls, Ceilings and Floors **140**
alcohol 35, 37, **53**, **57**
almonds 14, 27, 28
apple 17, **34**, 37, **39**
apple juice 56
apple pie 93, **120**, **126**
apricot 16, 27, **34**, 50, **53**, 56
  jam 93
arrowroot 93
Asda **112**
asparagus 15, 16
aspic 79, 93
aubergine 15, 16
avocado 15, 25

B
bacon 2, 89, **95**, 110
baked bean 22, **27**, **34**, 55, **61**
baking powder 62, 63, 68
banana 17, **27**, 29, **34**, 37, 55
  pudding **61**
barley 12
batter 77
bean curry **61**
bean sprouts 15, 23, **61**, **103**
beans 13, **14**, 22
beef 2, 22, 43, 74, 75, **120**, **131**
  and chestnut casserole **68**
beer 44, 46
beetroot 15
bicarbonate of soda 62, 63
bilberry 17
Birds Eye **102**
biscuit 20, **39**, 56, 66, **67**, **68**, 79, **121**
black eye beans **27**, 13
blackberry 17
blackcurrant 17, 28
black pudding **95**
blueberry chutney **68**
blue cheese **45**, **104**
borlotti beans 13
bouillon mix **68**
Bramleys Coffee House **68**
bran 23
bran cereal 52
brazil nuts 14, 27
bread 13, 20, 23, **27**, **34**, 36, 44, 55, **56**, 59, 62, 65, **69**, 74, 116, 117, **118**, **119**, **120**, 124, **129**
  and butter pudding **61**
  part baked 110
  wholemeal **34**, 55, **56**
Breadwinner Foods **108**
breakfast cereals **25**, **27**, **52**, 55, 56, 108, **110**, **120**
  wholemeal 56
Brie 10, **36**
British Bakeries **69**
broad beans 13, 15, **95**
broccoli 15, 16, **27**, **61**, **75**, **126**
  mornay **126**
brussels sprouts 15, **27**
burgers 37, **39**, **44**, 62, **71**, 74, 80, 89, **103**, **107**
butter 10-11, 18, 19, **26**, 27, 66, **70**, 131
butter beans 13, **14**, 15, **68**
buttercream 80
butterfly cakes **78**
buttermilk 11

C
cabbage 15
Cadbury **113**
cakes 20, 66-7, 74, 114, **118**, **119**, **120**, **123**, **124**, **136**
cannellini beans 13
cardoon 15
carrot **14**, 15, 16, 27, **39**, 55, **56**, **76**, **104**, **126**
cashews 14
Cauldron Foods **103**
cauliflower 15, 16, **61**
celeriac 15
celery 15, 55
ceps 15
cereals (also see breakfast cereals) 12-**13**, 25, 27, 28, 29, 43, 109, **120**
chanterellles 15
chapatti 35
Cheddar cheese 10, **11**, **36**, **64**, **84**
cheese 10, **11**, 22, **34**, **39**, **45**, **54**, **56**, **61**, 62, 70, 78, **80**, 90, **104**, **110**, **120**, **128**
  and tomato bread **118**
  sauce 62, **67**, **86**
  scones **61**
cheesecake **78**, **120**
cherry 16
  pie filling **68**
chestnut purée 14
chestnuts 14, **68**
chick peas 13, 22, **27**
chicken 2, **3**, 35, 42, 43, **44**, **76**, **107**, **126**, **136**, **137**
  curry **34**
  Kiev **107**
  liver **95**
  tikka **120**
  vol-au-vents **78**
chicory 15
chilli 74
chips **39**, 55, 56, **65**, **75**, 77, **86**, 89
Chinese leaves 15
chocolate 38, **39**, 56, 64, 100, **113**, **121**, **130**
  drinking chocolate 110
  eclair 109
  sponge **39**
chutney 20, **36**, **68**
ciabatta **84**
citrus fruits 17, 28
clarified butter 10
clementine 17
coconut 14, 56, **68**
coconut milk 14
coconut oil 25
cod **4**, **60**
coffee 47, 110, **120**
cola **39**, **56**, **59**, **97**
coleslaw 47
concentrated butter 11
coriander 62
corn 59
corn flakes 108, **112**
corn on the cob 16, **34**, **47**, 74, **86**
cornflour 59, 62, **68**
Cornish pasty 93, **126**, **127**
cottage cheese 10, **36**, 70
courgette 15, 16
crab 4
cranberry relish **86**
cream 9, **26**, 42, 70, 80, 81, 100
cream crackers **61**
crème brûlée 20
crème caramel 76
crème fraîche 70
croissant **68**
crumble
  fruit **61**
  mix 62
  vegetable **61**
  crumpets **61**
crisps 38, **39**, 51, 99, **104**, **110**, **112**, **115**
cucumber 15
cumberland sauce **68**, **95**
curry 74, **102**, **104**, **120**
custard 20, **39**, **61**, **68**, 74
  ready to serve 62

D
dairy products 8, **9**, **10**, **11**, 28, 29, 35, 36, 37, 42, **61**
damson 16
Dansco **11**
date 17, 56
deer 2
demerara sugar 20, 21
digestive biscuits **68**, **112**
doughnuts 74, 117, 118, 119
dried apricots 27, **34**, 50, **53**, 56
dried fruit 28, 29, 55, 56,
dried fruits 17
dried peaches 27
duck 2
Dutch brown beans 13

E
Edam 70
eggs 5-**6**, **7**, **14**, 22, 25, **27**, 28, 29, **34**, 35, 37, 42, **44**, 59, 66, 67, 73, 74, 75, 78, 89
  dried eggs 63
  glaze 93
  mayonnaise **120**
  Scotch 74
Elro **94**

F
Farm Produce Marketing **53**
feta cheese **36**
fig 17, 28, **34**, 56
Film Cuisine **120**
fish 3, **4**, **5**, 22, 25, **27**, 28, 29, **35**, 37, 42, 43, 46, 47, 59, **60**, **61**, **71**, 74, **76**, 89, 90, **104**, **107**, 110, **120**
  cakes 74, **75**
  fingers 37, **102**
  mornay **39**
  oils 18, 25, 27
flageolet beans 13
flapjacks **68**
flour 12, 44, 55, 59, 62, 65, 66, 67, **69**, **70**, 77, **121**, **128**, **129**
  chestnut 59
  corn 59, 62
  rice 59, **61**
  soya 59, **61**
  white 12, **69**, 70
  wholemeal 12, 55, **69**, 70
fromage frais 55, 70
fruit 16-**17**, 23, **34**, **36**, 37, 46, 48, **53**, 55, 56, 62, 70, 74, **80**, 109, **120**
  and nut flapjacks **68**
  cake 106, **118**
  flan 93
  fool **103**

G
gammon **86**
garlic 15, 62, **76**, **95**
  bread **36**
  purée **68**
gâteau 100, 109, **118**, **119**, **120**

gelatine 35, 62, 93
ghee **11**, 35, **55**
ginger **76**
  gingerbread 20, 66, 114, 115
  ginger cake 74
girolles 15
globe artichokes 15
goat's cheese **95**
golden syrup 20, 21
goose 2
goulash 74
grape 17
grapefruit 17
gravy 42, **86**
Green Meadow Foods **84**
green peppers **14**, 28
green vegetables 27, 28
groundnut oil 35
guava 17

H
haddock 4
halibut 4
ham **36**, 46, **95**, **120**
haricot beans 13, **14**
hazelnuts 14
Heathcotes Brasserie **95**
Heinz 30
herbal tea **54**
herbs 35, 62, 73
  dried **70**
herring 4
Heygates **129**
honey 70
hot cross buns 93
horseradish 15

I
ice cream 20, 43, 56, 89
Iceland **112**
icing 80, 114
  ready to roll 62
  sugar 20, 21

J
jam 20, 44, **56**, 74
  tarts **78**
jelly **39**, **104**, **110**
Jerusalem artichoke 15

K
kebab 74, 100, **103**
Kellogg's **112**
kidney 2
kidney beans 13, **68**
kippers 46
kiwi fruit 17
kohlrabi 15
kumquat 17
Kwik Save **112**

L
lamb 2, **3**, **70**, 74, 83
Lancashire cheese 10, **36**
lard 18, 19, **26**, **55**
lasagne **61**, **75**
leafy vegetables 28, 29
leek 15, 16, **75**
lemon 17
  juice 62, 66
  meringue pie **104**, **123**
  mousse **104**
lentil 13, **14**, **61**
  shepherd's pie **61**
lettuce 15
lima beans 15
lime 17
liver 22, 27, 28

141

Product and business index

lobster 4
low calorie drinks 56, **59**
low fat
    cheese 55
    cream 70
    spreads 18, **19**, **60**, 70
lychee 17

M
macadamia nuts 14
macaroni cheese **61**
mackerel **4**, **36**
maize 12, 20, 35
mandarin 17
    gâteau 120
mange tout peas 15, **76**
mango 17, 27
    chutney **68**
margarine 18, **19**, 28, **60**, 66, 67, 98
Marlow Foods Ltd 30
marrow 15
marrow fat peas 13
mayonnaise 42, **68**
McCain **128**
McVities **112**, **121**
meat **2-3**, 22, 25, 27, 28, 29, 35, 37, 40, 42, 43, 44, 46, 55, 62, **71**, 74, 75, 76, 77, 82, 89, 90, 100, **107**, 110, **120**, 127, 138
meatballs 100
melon **120**
meringues 20, 76, **78**, 100, 101
milk **8-9**, 22, **27**, 29, **34**, 35, 42, 43, 47, **52**, **53**, 55, 56, 59, 62, **64**, **70**, 110, **115**, **120**, **121**
    glaze 93
    milkshake 39
Milk Marque **53**
minestrone 106
molasses 20, 21
mooli 15
morels 15
mousse 42
mozarella **11**, **84**
mung beans 13
mushroom 15, 16, 27, **34**
    and walnut crêpes 100
    korma 120
    pâté **61**
    soup 115
mustard and cress 15
mustard oil 35
mutton 2, 35
mycoprotein (Quorn) 23, **30**

N
nectarine 17
nuts **14**, 22, 25, 28, 29, **34**, **36**, 37, 55, 56, 59, **68**

O
oat crackers **61**
oats 12, 23
offal 74
oil 18, 19, 25, **121**, **125**
    fish 18, 25, 27
    olive 18, **19**, 25, **55**
    rapeseed 55
    sunflower **55**
    vegetable 18, **19**, 25, 28, **55**
oily fish 3, **4**, 36
okara **103**
okra 15, **27**
Olestra 99
olive 25, **36**, 62, **128**
    tapenade **95**
omelette **126**
onion 14, 15, 16, 48, **70**, 75, **76**, 84
    rings 74
    stilton and leek tart **95**
orange 17, **27**, 55
orange juice **39**, **109**
orange squash **105**
ostrich 2
oyster mushrooms 15

oysters 4

P
palm oil 25
papaya 17
Parkwood House Day Nursery **61**
parrot fish 4
parsley 28, 62
    dried **68**
parsnip 15, 16
passion fruit 17
pasta 30, 36, 59, 62, 74, 80, 81, **85**, **102**, 110, 115
pasties 93, **103**, 106, 126, 127
pastry 62, 65, 66, **67**, 74, 78, 79, 80, 93, **95**, **102**, **127**
    frozen 62
pâté 36, **103**
peach 17, 27
peanut butter 14
peanuts 14, 22, 27, 55,
pear 17, **34**
peas 15, **27**, **39**, **86**, **127**
    frozen 102
pecans 14
pepper 62, 68
pepperoni **128**
peppers 15, 16, 28, 74
    stuffed with spinach and ricotta 100
pheasant 2
pickle 36, 46
pie **89**, **102**, 106
pie filling 62, 68
pineapple 17, **86**
    tinned **68**
pinto beans 13
pistachios 14
pitta bread **34**
pizza 34, 39, 47, 56, 62, 75, **78**, 118, **119**, **128**
pizza base mix 62
plaice 4
plantain 35
plum 7
poppadoms 110
pork 2, 35, 71, 74
pork pie 138
porridge 56, **120**
porridge oats **14**
potato 15, **16**, 22, 23, **27**, 28, 36, 42, 43, 47, 48, 55, 56, 59, **64**, **70**, 73, 74, 75, 80, 81, **86**, **120**, **126**
poultry 2, 3, 40, 42, 43, 55, 74
prawn **36**
prawn cocktail 4
preserves 20, 46
preserving sugar 20, 21
pulses 13, **14**, 22, 27, 28, 29, 35, 37, 56, 59, **61**
pumpkin 15, 16
pumpkin seeds 14

Q
quail 2
Quark 70
quiche **61**
Quorn (mycoprotein) 23, **30**, 71

R
rabbit 2
radiccio 15
radish 15, 55
raisins 17, **34**
Rank Hovis McDougall 30
raspberry 17
ratatouille 74
ravioli 74
redcurrant 17
redcurrant jelly 93
red peppers 28
rennet 11, 35
rice 12, 22, 23, **27**, 35, **39**, 42, 43, 48, 55, 56, 59, 74
rice crackers **61**

rice pudding **61**, **104**
rock cakes 66
rocket 15
Roquefort 10
roux sauce **13**, **67**
runner beans 15
rye 12

S
Safeway **45**, **112**
Sainsbury **112**
salad 36, **39**, 42, 47, **109**, 115, **120**
salad dressing 18, 36, 42, **68**, **103**, **125**
salmon 4, **93**
salsify 15
salt 29, 35, 37, 56, **57**, 62, **68**, **69**, 70, 71, 99
sandwiches 47, **61**, 81, **84**, **106**, **109**, **120**, **126**
sardines **34**, **61**
sauce 42, **67**, 74, **110**
sausages 22, 37, **44**, 47, 71, 74, 80, 81, **89**, **103**
scampi **107**
scones **78**, 93, **120**
sea kale 15
sea vegetables 23, 28, 29
seafood 4, 29, 42
seeds 14, 28, 29, 37
sesame seeds 14, **61**
shallot 15
shepherd's pie 80, **107**
shellfish 4, 35, 42, 59, 74
shortbread 67, **104**
shrimp 42
smetana 11
smoked
    fish **4**, **36**, 43
    haddock **120**
    ham **84**
soft cheese **43**, **45**
soft drinks **39**, **53**, 56, **59**, **89**, **96**, **97**, **98**, **105**
soft fruits 17
soissons 13
sole 4
sorbet 47
sorrel 15
soup 42, **46**, **61**, **68**, 106, 115, **120**
soya
    beans 13, 23, **27**, 59, **103**
    'cheese' **103**
    flour **103**
    'milk' 22, **61**, **103**
soy sauce **103**
spaghetti 30, **110**
spices 35, 48, 62, 73, **76**, **128**
spinach 15, **27**, 28
split peas 13
sponge
    cake **104**
    layers **68**
    pudding 74
spring onion 15
squash 15
steak and kidney pie 93
sticky toffee pudding **68**
stir-fried
    rice **34**
    tofu **103**
    vegetables **61**
stock 56, 62, **63**, **70**
strawberry 17, 28, 131
strawberry dessert 50
suet 66
    puddings 74
sugar 20, **21**, 23-24, 36, 37, 44, 56, 66, 67, 70, 71, 99, **121**
    and water glaze 93
    brown 20, 21
sultana **68**
sun dried tomato pâté **84**
sunflower seeds 14
swede 15

sweet potatoes 16, 27, 35
sweetcorn 15, 55, **68**
sweets 56
Swiss chard 15
Swiss roll 66
syrup 74

T
tahini 14
tangerine 17
tarragon **95**
tea 29, **39**, **112**, **120**
terrine **95**
Tesco **60**, **108**, **112**
textured vegetable protein (TVP) 23, **103**
tinned fruit **39**
tiramisu **68**
toast 81, **120**
toffee **104**
tofu 22, 28, **47**, **103**, **104**
tomato 15, 20, 27, 28, **34**
    purée 62
    sauce 62
    soup **68**, **78**, 106
    tinned 62, 68, **128**
    vinaigrette **95**
treacle 20, 21
trifle **78**
tropical fruits 17
trout **4**, 14
tuna **36**, 42, **61**, **68**, **120**
    and bean salad **68**
    and pasta bake 115
turkey 2
turnip 15

U
ugli fruit 17
United Biscuits **121**

V
vanilla essence 62
veal 100

vegetable 16, 23, 27, 28, 29, 36, 37, 43, 46, **53**, **54**, 55, 56, **61**, 62, **71**, 73, 74, 75, **76**, **77**, **80**, **89**, **93**, **95**, 100, **102**, **120**, 127
    balti **120**
    chilli tacos **120**
    lasagne **68**
    moussaka **39**
vegetable oil 18, 19, 25, 28, **55**
vegetarian
    burgers **47**
    cottage pie **86**, **103**
venison 2
Victoria sandwich 66, 79, 80
vinaigrette **36**
vinegar **44**, 62, **125**

W
Walkers **112**
walnut 14
    pesto **95**
watercress 15, 27, **93**
wheat 12, 20, 48, 62, **129**
wheatgerm 27, 28, 56, **61**
white fats 18, **55**
white fish 4
wine 46, **70**, 90

Y
yam 15, 35
yeast 27, 65, **69**, **128**
yeast extract 22, **27**, 29, **34**, **61**, 62
yogurt 9, **10**, **27**, **34**, **39**, 40, 51, **54**, 55, **61**, 62, **101**, 131